Parent's

Guide to Being a Mum

I'M SORRY - I JUST DON'T BELIEVE THAT YOU EXIST...

LOCH NESS MONSTER

Perfect MUM

The **Paren**talk Parenting Course

Helping you to be a Better Parent

Being a parent is not easy. **Parentalk** is a new, video-led, parenting course designed to give groups of parents the opportunity to share their experiences, learn from each other and discover some principles of parenting. It is suitable for anyone who is a parent or is planning to become a parent.

The Parentalk Parenting Course features:

Steve Chalke – TV Presenter; author on parenting and family issues; father of four and **Parentalk** Chairman.

Rob Parsons – author of *The Sixty Minute Father* and *The Sixty Minute Mother*; and Executive Director of Care for the Family.

Dr Caroline Dickinson – inner city-based GP and specialist in obstetrics, gynaecology and paediatrics.

Kate Robbins – well-known actress and comedienne.

Each **Parentalk** session is packed with group activities and discussion starters.

Made up of eight sessions, the **Parentalk** Parenting Course is easy to use and includes everything you need to host a group of up to ten parents.

Each Parentalk Course Pack contains:
- A **Parentalk** video
- Extensive, easy-to-use, group leader's guide
- Ten copies of the full-colour course material for members
- Photocopiable sheets/OHP masters

Price £49.95

Additional participant materials are available so that the course can be run again and again.

To order your copy, or to find out more, please contact:

Parentalk

PO Box 23142, London SE1 0ZT
Tel: 020 7450 9073
Fax: 020 7450 9060
e-mail: info@parentalk.co.uk

The **Paren**talk Guide to Being a Mum

Janice Fixter

Series Editor: Steve Chalke

Illustrated by John Byrne

Hodder & Stoughton
LONDON SYDNEY AUCKLAND

For Amy, Ellie, Benjamin and Joseph
who have promised to help me look for the rest
of my marbles

British Library Cataloguing in Publication Data
A record for this book is available from the British Library

ISBN 0 340 75656 X

Typeset by Avon Dataset Ltd, Bidford-on-Avon, Warks

Printed and bound in Great Britain by
Clays Ltd, St Ives plc

Hodder and Stoughton Ltd
A Division of Hodder Headline
338 Euston Road
London NW1 3BH

Contents

Acknowledgements

I'd like to thank Mike, my husband, who provided much patience and many takeaways, and without whom this book would not have been written. I'd also like to thank Gill Dutton for her support and encouragement, and Sue Young for her valuable insight. I'm grateful to the many mums who took the time to talk to me about their experiences, and to Tim Mungeam for his painstaking reading of the final manuscript.

Real Mums Wear Dribble

What Should I Expect as a Mum?

It's 4.30 p.m. and I'm in the kitchen trying to work out what to give the children for tea while answering strange questions about Henry VIII and his numerous wives, looking for lines of symmetry in a piece of maths homework, organising who watches what on the TV and explaining why my decision is fair. And it's only Monday.

I'm pretty certain that this sort of scene is repeated in thousands of homes across the country at the same time every day. When I had my first child I had no idea that a relatively quiet life would turn out like this! If every mother was endowed with the gift of hindsight on the arrival of their first born, being a mum would be so much easier, or alternatively it would mean that first babies remained only children. Instead the baby arrives with clenched little fists and a helpless gaze and in that moment, whether you're prepared or not, you've got the role of 'responsible adult'. Before you even start to grapple with

1

that idea, you're swamped with nappies, toothy grins, first day at school, and suddenly there you are standing in the kitchen contemplating burgers and chips and why Henry had so many wives called Catherine. And it all happens so quickly that you barely have time to sit down and think about what you're doing. Then someone suddenly calls out that well-known name 'Mum . . .'

My friend Beth, who has teenage children, tells me that the best preparation for motherhood is working on a farm – early mornings, mucking out, strange smells and never a day off. But there are high expectations of mums at the beginning of the twenty-first century. We're surrounded by images of the perfect mum in magazines and on the television. She's always smiling, has shiny hair and sparkling teeth and she's regained her figure just weeks after childbirth. Her baby gurgles happily, wears nappies that never leak and goes to sleep on white fluffy sheets without hours of back-patting. The perfect mother would never have a baby that preferred to tip a bowl of spaghetti bolognese over its head rather than eat it. Neither would she seal her child into its nappy with half a roll of sticky tape because she's smeared the original tapes with zinc and castor oil cream.

 Top Tip: *Remember that the perfect mum is a figment of your imagination.*

Advertisers don't show you photos of real mums – you know the ones with designer bags under their eyes and dribble on their shoulder; the ones who are too tired to take up aerobics, never buy clothes that are 'hand wash only' or 'please iron' and who believe a good night's sleep is the best surprise birthday present they could ever have. The only consolation is that, in real life, the image of an ideal mum is easily shattered.

Dispelling the Myth

At a school sports day the mums lined up, a mixture of eagerness and terror, to do their best in the Mums' Race. Most appeared totally unprepared to sprint and were dressed in typical school-run wear. There was one mum, however, who was clearly a cut above the rest, in the sports' wear department anyway. She was wearing a sports top, tracksuit trousers and running shoes. It was obvious, looking at her, that no one stood a chance. And indeed they didn't. From the word go she led the pack and by the half-way line she was unbeatable. However, just a few metres before the finish, disaster struck and, much to the delight of the school children and the horror of the teachers, the elastic in her trousers gave way. She was over the line first, but what she will be remembered for is not the glorious victory but the pair of knickers that were too skimpy to hide her embarrassment!

There is no such thing as the perfect mother, in the same way as there's no such thing as a perfect child, but it's easy to be seduced into the romantic glow of motherhood. However, the reality of day-to-day life with children is far from romantic. Children make demands on their parents from the moment they're born: crying, screaming, interrupting, attention-seeking.

3

We can end up so busy responding to those demands that we forget to sit down and do what really matters which is to show our children we love them. And doing that takes time and sometimes effort. It takes both if you're faced with a seven-year-old who wants to give you a blow-by-blow account of what went on in the playground at lunch time. Children do not quantify their parents' love by the number of treats they get or the number of after-school activities their mums take them to; children understand love by the amount of time their parents spend talking to them and, above all, the time they spend listening to them.

> **Top Tip:** *Investing as much time as you possibly can in your children is the best way to show you love them.*

Rachel was desperate to get it right and become a good mother. She wanted to do the best she could for her son, so she read every parenting magazine that was around and all the child-care books she could lay her hands on. One magazine in particular told her that babies need constant stimulation and that 'good' mothers achieve this by rotating the baby's toys on a weekly basis. Rachel thought this sounded like a great idea, one that was nice and methodical instead of a bit airy fairy. She made a list of every toy her son had and drew neat columns so she could tick off each toy on a weekly basis. By this rotational system Rachel could ensure that Mark had the constant stimulation he required and all she had to do was keep on top of the paperwork. While there's nothing wrong with the idea of changing toys around, Rachel didn't see, at first, that the most important source of stimulation for Mark was not the revolving toys – here one week, gone the next – but the time she spent with her son, talking and playing with him. Being a good mum isn't about keeping a checklist, it's about spending time with your child – talking, listening and playing together.

We're surrounded by small print. Buy a house, rent a flat, open a bank account, rush into the sales for a special offer and you'll see a sign in minuscule writing which states 'terms and conditions apply'. When you become a mum – perhaps the biggest investment you'll ever make – there are no terms or conditions. Having a child means making 'daily payments', not in money terms (although children don't come cheap) but rather in unconditional love. This is the best investment you can make: the kind of love that isn't dependent on what she says or does; the kind of love that doesn't say 'I love you as long as you . . .', but instead embraces the child, faults, grubby fingers and all; the kind of love that separates the behaviour from the person. Children who grow up in such an environment will grow into secure adults.

Don't be conned either into thinking that the ideal mum is the one who can cope with hoards of her child's friends round every day or who can afford to send her child to after-school activities three times a week. Sometimes the pressure of rushing around adds to the stress of everyday life. Children get as tired as adults with all the hubbub, and spending some time at home is as good for them as it is for us. What's even better is when your child spends time at home with *you* – talking and listening.

The Secret of Success

Not only are we pounded with images of how the 'good' mum looks but also how she makes the perfect choices for her child. And it's true that from the moment the pregnancy test kit gives you the happy news you're bombarded with hundreds of choices: about where and how to have your baby, which nappy to use, when to wean, whether to buy baby food or make it at home, the best way to potty train, which pre-school, which primary school, which secondary school, whether to let him play computer games for hours on end – the list is endless. And all these decisions are yours, along with your partner if you have one, or whoever you trust to help you make choices. At the end of the day many of the options you are faced with are hardly life-changing, so don't spend too much time worrying about them. Don't spend sleepless nights fretting about whether you're feeding your child with the best baby food – it doesn't matter what brand of baby food you buy as long as it gets eaten!

 Top Tip: *Listen to well-meaning advice but don't feel obliged to take it!*

It's amazing how many people are willing to share with you the secret of success. They'll happily spend hours telling you how they got it right and as a consequence little Johnny never cried, was walking by the age of nine months and went to university at fifteen. This serves no purpose other than to unintentionally make you feel inadequate before your baby is three months old. People mean well, but as every mother has a different story and often gives different advice you can be left feeling bewildered, at best. It seems that everybody's child except yours was out of nappies by eighteen months and never made puddles on the neighbour's carpet. This can be particularly demoralising when you've just spent the whole summer chasing your toddler with a potty and a disinfectant spray and have become incapable of holding an uninterrupted conversation.

Percolated or Filtered?

Mums whose babies have long since grown up frequently have memories like coffee filters. The good stuff drains through while the grouts of reality are screwed up and thrown in the bin, or if you're environmentally conscious they're put on the compost heap to be recycled. Either way it's selective memory at work, so don't believe everything you hear. The summers were always hotter and the sky was always bluer. And remember there will always be a David's mum who bakes her own bread and would never fall foul of an empty fridge on a Friday night and end up in the chippy; or a Kirsty's mum who gives her children real puddings every day instead of yoghurt and bananas. So don't judge yourself by other people's standards.

Right from the beginning it's important to know that *you* are the ideal person to look after your child and make choices for her – no matter what your mother-in-law may tell you! You know your child far better than anyone else and you're in a unique position to understand her. What works for one parent may not work for another, so don't be fooled into thinking you're a failure because your best friend's advice didn't work immediately. What's important is that children feel loved and secure, and you can do that by regularly giving them your undivided attention and by frequently telling them that you love them – and that's as important to teenagers as it is to toddlers. A child knows when you're not really listening, when you've got one eye on the clock and you're making noncommittal noises such as 'mmm, that's nice, dear'. Remember that children learn by example and you could end up in the situation one day where it's you who wants some attention but instead your son or daughter just mutters incoherent reassuring noises a foot over *your* head!

Top Tip: *Start telling your son or daughter that you love them and don't stop – even when they're bigger than you!*

While people will queue to tell you they did it their way and it worked, not many people will tell you that they blew it! Few will tell you that, as a mum, you will make mistakes and however hard you try you will not be the perfect mother. Inevitably we all have the capacity to make wrong judgments or lose our tempers. It's hard to believe that you'll shout at your baby when she's sleeping like an angel but when toddling Hannah has been creative on the wallpaper with a big box of crayons – again – tempers get frayed: and we are all capable of overreacting or blaming children for something that's not their fault. I used to frown at mothers who shouted at children in supermarkets or yelled in the middle of shopping centres. I feel more sympathetic now, especially after the day we went shopping and Benjamin, having insisted on carrying his new school shoes, got back to the car without them. I was so furious that I jumped up and down in the middle of the car park like a demented kangaroo. (Much to everyone's relief we eventually discovered the abandoned shoes in a coffee shop so we were able to go home smiling – albeit through gritted teeth.)

How the Mighty Have Fallen

Not only are we all capable of losing our rag, but, with the best will in the world, we can all make wrong decisions. When our eldest daughter Amy was about a year old we went away on holiday to Yorkshire. It was one of those really glorious weeks and what better way to cool down than to buy some ice cream? We bought three and gave our daughter her very first vanilla cone. At that time I was still hanging on to the ideal that good mums have clean children. I was never going to be one of those mothers whose children had runny noses and dirty faces. And although it was her first ice cream time, I was ready with a handful of tissues and baby wipes to mop up any spillage. After all, if you teach them how to eat properly when they're babies they'll always be clean and tidy eaters – or so I thought.

Amy loved this treat and it wasn't long before she was up to her nose in a melting, gooey mess. It was clear that tissues weren't going to do enough damage limitation so the only alternative was to take the ice cream away. Have you ever tried removing a one-year-old from her ice cream once she's got hold of it? Amy wasn't happy, and neither would I have been in her shoes, and having the upper hand she decided there was only one way to stop me stealing this wonderful stuff, which was by hiding the ice cream up her dress – which she did, very successfully.

Top Tip: *Don't worry about making mistakes but make your mind up to learn from them.*

Before I had children I had a great many ideals. During pregnancy, in particular, I would watch mums with their children and make mental notes about what they were doing wrong. It's easy to judge when your baby's little more than a butterfly bump. The world can be neatly divided into two: those who don't have children but who know exactly the correct way of raising pillars of society, and those who have children and haven't got a clue if they're doing it right. It didn't take long for me to pack up my ideals and change camps. Nowadays you only have to peer through the letterbox of our house any school day at 8.30 a.m. to appreciate imperfect mothering. If I was a little more organised and took account of the fact that my children would really rather spend the day at home in front of the TV/playing football/listening to the radio then I would be less surprised when no one is ready to leave on time. I end up shouting as we play 'Hunt the Shoe'. We all know that the shoe was by the front door at eight o'clock but somehow, now it's needed, it has mysteriously disappeared without trace. Or there's the game of 'What have you done with your homework?' – very popular on a Monday morning when Benjamin has had a whole weekend to forget where he put it.

Mums do not want to send their children to school after they've shouted and screamed: they do not want their children to arrive at school upset and with faces like thunder. I, for one, want to be one of those mothers who smiles serenely at her children as they line up to leave the house in an ordered fashion (do they really exist?). I do not want to attempt to remove small splatterings of chocolate spread from my son's school sweatshirt as we hurry down the road. I do not want to discover, as we walk through the school gate, that two of my children, in spite of repeated instructions, have not cleaned their teeth (the only real, if a little regimental, solution to this problem is a teeth inspection *before* you leave the house). The only consolation is that when I get to school I meet other mums who are just as fraught as I am and it's very comforting to realise that so many of us are in the same unsteady boat. So don't panic and think you're the only mum in the world who feels incapable of controlling their child. Even top city executives who once organised teams of people can be reduced to chasing their children out of the front door in the morning like juvenile sheep dogs. Remember that it's a fact of life that things get lost (including tempers) and it's quite normal to feel as if you're losing control of a runaway train. In reality, you're doing what every other mum has ever done – doing your best.

 Top Tip: *On the days that both you and your child run smoothly, wallow in the feeling and dish out bucketfuls of praise.*

Learning Curves in All the Wrong Places

Being a mum means living on an accelerated learning curve, enjoying the occasional success but mainly learning from your mistakes. From day one you start learning about the little individual who's been entrusted into your care, a person that you know nothing about. You may have chosen the father, possibly with rose-coloured glasses and stars in your eyes, but you have no choice about the sort of baby you will have! And, despite all the wonderful advice about eating sugary or acidic foods or running round the garden three times clockwise under a full moon, there is no real way to ensure that you'll have a boy or a girl, let alone choose their disposition. And there is so much to learn about your child that it can seem a monumental task.

Every age group is full of surprises. The child development books may give you a rough idea of what will happen at a certain age but the theory of 'starts to walk unaided' is often very different from the practice. I sometimes think it would be more useful to know at what stage of development you have to move everything three feet up or lock your most precious ornaments in a cupboard. It helps if you get to know children who are older than yours, children who are a stage or two ahead; then you've got an idea of what's coming next. You can learn an enormous amount from parents of older children. Other mums will tell you exactly what to expect when your baby starts crawling and your home goes from being a safe environment to the equivalent of a munitions factory overnight. Find out how other mums cope with the problems you've yet to face and stash the knowledge in reserve for when your time comes. Keep in mind that no mother is expected to be an expert straight away. Instead expect to be always travelling but never arriving. Mums learn in small stages – any quicker would probably be detrimental to our health! And just when you think you've got something right – when you're feeling pleased with the way you've handled a difficult situation – remember the proverb of pride before a fall.

SO FAR SHE'S BROKEN TWO CUPS, THE VIDEO AND MY ROSE COLOURED GLASSES ..

Top Tip: Don't be afraid to ask other mums how they cope with a particular problem. You may be amazed at how many solutions there are.

Animal Crackers

Also be mindful of the maxim about not working with children and animals. We've had a whole stream of small creatures through our house over the years. The small furry kind have a short life-span, so we've had many hamsters and gerbils, sometimes more than intended when two 'females' have produced a litter. I always thought that when these small animals moved on to the big hamster/gerbil cage in the sky, it was a good opportunity to talk to the children about life and death in a way they could understand. Knowing that one of our hamsters called Woody (in pre *Toy Story* days) was on her last legs, I broached the subject with the children and explained that Woody wouldn't be with us for much longer. Sure enough, a couple of days later she died, just before we went on holiday. We had a very solemn ceremony in the garden, where we buried her, and placed a paving slab on top of the grave to keep the foxes out.

For years I thought I'd handled this well until one day Amy finally told me that her recollection of the story was quite different. She had no idea that the hamster had died and hadn't got a clue what I was talking about. Bearing in mind that she's a very bright girl I have to assume that I was at fault here. Amy, who was about three at the time, thought that we'd buried the hamster in the garden because we were going on holiday. She thought this was very strange as all her friends at school moved their hamsters to someone else's home while they were away, but not us; we buried ours in the garden and put a big heavy stone on top for good measure to make sure the hamster couldn't get out! To make matters worse, she also believed that we intended to dig up Woody when we returned and we would all be reunited as one big happy family. Of course, we didn't dig Woody up when we got home and this puzzled Amy for a long time – but she didn't mention it to us until years later!

So much for good communication with our children. So be

warned, your children may hear what you say, but have no idea what you mean. Of course the other problem is that you can be sure, whether they understand it or not, they will gleefully echo to all and sundry the very words you don't want them to repeat such as 'My mummy says your dog looks like a bog brush'. So if you don't want it repeated to Granny, Uncle Steve or the lady in the sweet shop, don't say it!

Top Tip: *If you don't want it repeated to all and sundry – don't say it in front of the children!*

Then there's the minefield of social development to wade through. Thanks to Freud and his friends there's a great deal of knowledge or supposition about what happens if your child gets stuck in some phase or other; and none of us want our children to end up with strange complexes. Children constantly move towards independence and maturity and it's primarily the parent's job to encourage them in the right direction, rather than forever treat them as children. Take an interest in your child's character and see her strengths as well as weaknesses. Help her to make the most of what she's good at: encourage her to work at areas she struggles with. Your child may never be a Carol Vorderman but it doesn't mean she should skip learning her times tables. Don't give your child a label such as 'the clever one' or 'the stupid one' – labels can tend to stick. They either drive the child into the ground as she tries to live up to them or give her nothing to aim for. After all, if your mum says you're stupid what's the point in bothering?

Sense of Humour Test

The most important thing you should learn to hang on to, right from the beginning, is your sense of humour; and if you haven't got one already, get one quick! Don't take yourself too seriously. How else can you cope with the toddler who tugs frantically at your knees in Marks and Spencer demanding the toilet *after* her wellington boots have overflowed in the middle of ladies' nightwear? How else do you react when your child brings you a gift of the most enormous wriggly worm she could find in the garden and places it firmly in your unsuspecting hand? Laughing with your children dispels tension and can completely change the atmosphere in a home, so do it often.

Some of our mistakes are a real tonic. Our daughter, aged six, was asked to draw a picture of as many words beginning with 'ch' as she could think of. One of her pictures was of three little faces with the word 'chiplets' written underneath. We explained to her why it was amusing and after that, for quite a while, chiplets became part of the family vocabulary. It's easy to get discouraged but laughing with each other helps to keep a sense of perspective and can make a huge difference to your sanity.

Top Tip: *Try to hang onto your sense of humour even if everything else has deserted you – it'll help you to keep things in perspective.*

Once she reaches school you'll need a sense of humour just to cope with the extra demands your child will place upon you. No one told me I'd end up spending hours in the library searching for obscure books before organising my ten-year-old so she can manage twelve pages on the Yangtze River. Nor did they tell me that I would end up digging through twenty years of memory in a vain attempt to conjugate a French irregular verb in order to help my twelve-year-old with her homework; while she, of course, stands there looking at me as if *I'm* the one speaking a foreign language because they don't learn French like that any more. Neither is she, nor any of her friends, impressed by the fact that I can say 'the dog is in the street' in Latin.

Before I became a mum I didn't realise that children expect their mums to have the mental capacity of a Pentium III computer with 128 megabytes of random access memory and no room for lost files or hardware failure. My mother never told me I'd need four pairs of hands and the ability to mind read and see round corners. I frequently point out to my children that I'm a mum, not an octopus, and that my eyes do not pop out on stalks and extend fifty metres so they can peer into every room of the house. In spite of this they still try to overload me with lunch boxes and books or ask me to look at pictures they've drawn when I'm emptying the washing machine and they're in their bedroom. Children expect their mums to be miracle workers so don't be surprised when your child thinks you can do the impossible. Make the most of the fact that one person at least (and for the moment) thinks you're capable of anything – it's a big compliment!

Without a doubt, being a mum is an overwhelming experience. You're overwhelmed with joy as much as you are with the rollercoaster of exhaustion, frustration, worry and the big pile of washing that children create. But at the end of the day you'll suffer the uphill struggle willingly for the moment your child places a stalkless daisy in your hand and tells you she's picked it for you because she loves you.

Nappies, Nappies Everywhere . . .

How Do I Survive the First Months?

What do newborn babies have in common with rock stars? They both sleep during the day and stay up all night; they scream for attention; they're constantly drinking, and they have to be driven everywhere. Having a baby calls for Adjustment with a capital A: babies do not come with volume buttons or a battery compartment; you can't switch them off for a while when you've had enough. It's a twenty-four-hour-a-day, seven-days-a-week responsibility with no time off for sickness or holidays, and you can't even get parole for good behaviour! While there's so much to be done in practical terms before the big arrival – buying nappies, babygros, creams for a variety of ailments, not to mention a pram and a cot and a chair and a baby bath – what you're really preparing for is a giant step into the unknown with only a changing bag as a parachute. Until you've got your newborn in your arms you don't really know what you're letting yourself in for; and by the time you begin to realise, it's too late to do anything about it. I sometimes wonder what made Mike and me so sure we still wanted four children once we had one screaming baby. Had I lost my sanity in a fog of exhaustion, or was my midwife right when she said that half my brain cells had migrated to the placenta and would never be seen again? Whichever way you look at it you can't escape the fact that having a baby does strange things to you.

The last few sleepless months of pregnancy prepare the expectant mum for what is to come. The all-night parties are replaced by the all-night tossing and turning of a beached whale – a gentle warning that sleep has been reduced to the size of a minimum wage where it was once as large as a water company executive's salary. I would happily have throttled the mums who smugly told me that their babies slept through the night from two weeks – if I'd had the energy, that is! Looking in the mirror only confirmed that I was a bug-eyed monster, irrational with exhaustion. I'd gone from a twenty-something into an eighty-something overnight, with clothes that didn't fit in any of the right places, a washed-out complexion and remnants of a strange, waddling gait. After baby number one the midwife ordered rest, but I was so eager to get some control over my body and my life that I didn't take any notice – it's not just kids who don't do as they're told.

Jump Start or Recovery?

Mums don't always give themselves long enough to recover from childbirth. It takes more time than you think and it can take even longer if you've had a Caesarean section. My friend

Pauline ended up having three children by Caesarean and felt it would have been more practical if she'd had a zip put in first time round – it would have saved her a lot of recovery time and the need for subsequent anaesthetics.

No longer are mums expected to stay in hospital for several days, unless there have been complications; instead they can spend as little as a few hours as in-patients before rushing home. 'Childbirth is not an illness' we hear everyone say, so despite good advice about taking it easy and resting, lots of new mums feel duty-bound or well enough to be up and out within a week. I had three of my children at home and confess to being caught red-handed by the midwife on one occasion as I sprinted over the stair gate on my way back to bed on day two. But I have to say that rushing around like an Olympic athlete didn't do me any good at all.

 Top Tip: *Take every opportunity to rest and you'll feel more able to manage the demands of a small baby.*

The most important thing you can do to help yourself adjust to all the changes is to rest from the moment you have your baby. Give yourself time to recover fully and you'll be better equipped to cope – childbirth is an enormous upheaval, so don't expect to bounce back to full health and strength immediately. In some cultures women are taken good care of for up to forty days after the birth of their baby: local village women and female relatives all do their bit to give the mother a chance

23

to recuperate after delivery rather than encouraging her to rush back to normal as soon as possible (there are also cultures where the father gets put to bed and taken care of, but that's a different story altogether!). Of course, rest is easier with the first baby, by a mile. But it's as important, if not more so, to rest when you've got more than one child – take every opportunity, however snatched and short, to put your feet up and have a nap. Sleep when the baby sleeps. Don't feel guilty about it either. If you don't have the chance to sleep then learn to sit still for five minutes without jumping up and down (like a game of musical chairs) to check the baby's all right or to put another wash load on. Remember that 'normal' has now disappeared, for a while, over the horizon with its backside on fire, certainly as far as your body is concerned, so try to create opportunities for yourself to get your strength back.

Moonlight Becomes You, It Goes with Your Hair . . .

Most babies do not make a clear-cut distinction between night and day. No one told any of my babies that they were supposed to sleep when it's dark and be alert and mesmerising when the sun was shining. The books all tell you that new babies sleep for sixteen out of twenty-four hours a day, but which sixteen hours (and some sleep a great deal less than that) is a lottery: pick any sixteen from twenty-four. You may be fortunate enough to have a baby who nods off at eight o'clock in the evening and snoozes his way through the night, but if you haven't got a little angel you'll have to take steps to encourage good sleeping patterns. Think long term: the patterns you establish now will be hard for you to break when your child is two. We got into a terrible habit of swinging the carry cot in order to send our eldest to sleep. That was fine when she was seven pounds but by the time she was nearer twenty it was no joke. One night Mike suddenly came to his senses and realised quite how ridiculous the whole scenario had become and how many hours he had spent in this back-breaking position. That was the day we resolved to find another method of encouraging the baby to sleep – one that didn't require a course in body building!

 Top Tip: *Look for long-term solutions to sleeping problems – a quick fix may get you a couple of nights' sleep immediately but it often brings its own difficulties.*

If your baby is one of the many thousands who wake at night, aim to make night-time feeds and disturbances as boring as possible. Don't make them worth waking up for. It's best to avoid getting the toys out and playing peek-a-boo at 1.30 in the morning, even in desperation, or you may find a one-off develops into a habit. Handle your baby, feed him, change him, wind him, with the minimum of fuss and settle him down again as quickly as possible. Lots of babies fall asleep when they're feeding which means the baby never has a chance to fall asleep on his own. Once your baby gets to three months or so try putting him into the cot when he's drowsy rather than when he's already asleep; get him used to going to sleep on his own.

Older babies often develop comfort habits that help them get to sleep instead of being cuddled by you. Quilts, soft toys, blankets can all be used with a bit of encouragement. Give your baby a favourite soft toy whenever you put him to bed on his own. Some children suck their thumbs or dummies – in our house we had a hair twiddler: our second daughter Eleanor would fiddle with her hair (or anyone else's, given the chance) when she was drowsy. The big advantage of this was that we didn't have to cart anything extra round with us in order to get her to sleep. Haircuts were kept to a minimum and we had one thing less to remember to stuff into a changing bag already splitting at the seams.

Ooh, Aahh

If you're on your own don't be afraid to ask relatives and friends to take the baby off your hands to give you a break. An evening to yourself, even if it's spent sleeping, will do you good, so try to avoid the temptation of cramming fifteen different jobs into your couple of hours off. If you have a partner get him to give you a break whenever he can. A besotted dad oohing and aahing over the baby all the time is an asset to make the most of, so let him do some of the jigging around, back patting, trying to get the baby back to sleep routine. (In fact, anyone who offers to jiggle the baby for you should be invited round on a regular basis.) Don't be tempted always to take over because you've quickly learnt to be more adept – share baby care between you. We all have to start somewhere and if you never give your partner the chance to learn, you can't blame him when it seems to you that he can't get it right.

Eleanor did not sleep through the night until she was three. There were days when we were beside ourselves with exhaustion. The sometimes hourly waking was like water torture; just as we were drifting off she would start crying again and we would take it in turns to go to her. Friends, relatives and the doctor were full of ideas and advice and we tried the lot. We finally managed to get her into a reasonable sleep pattern by making a tape of music she seemed to respond to. It meant all we had to do was stagger out of bed several times during the night and hit the play button on the cassette recorder. No baby lullabies for us – we had to listen to the theme tune from *Neighbours* on the hour, every hour for about a week. It didn't solve the problem completely but it did reduce Eleanor's waking to once or twice a night and made life bearable. So be creative with your sleepless baby, consider all suggestions and then do whatever works for you.

 Top Tip: *Think about establishing a routine for your baby from early on – that way you both know what to expect and it will help you to make bedtimes as stress-free as possible.*

Cry Babies and Crooners

Then there's the daytime crying. When our youngest was born he yelled for a good hour and a half with his eyes clamped tightly shut. My dad came to visit and could hear him screaming half way down the road. Babies have only one way of communicating and that's by opening their mouth and making a noise. To start off with, all the cries sound the same, but after a bit of practice (of which you'll get plenty) you'll soon learn to recognise what some of the cries mean. At the beginning, however, you may just have to investigate every possibility when your baby cries and go through the rigmarole of whether he's hungry, windy, filling his nappy or needing a cuddle – all four tend to become inextricably linked in the end. Learn which position your baby is most comfortable in; some babies like to be soothed upright, others want to lay face down across your arm.

 Top Tip: *If you have a baby who is constantly crying, plan to give yourself a break when the baby settles, even if it's only for five minutes.*

And if you've gone through the lot and still can't calm your baby, try distracting him. When you're at your wits' end, or preferably before then, try it. Anything will do as long as it's safe.

- Stand in front of any moving object, such as the swinging pendulum of a clock.
- Fill the house with mobiles or wind chimes that dance in the breeze – they give your baby something to look at and listen to.
- Hang the washing out and walk round the washing line

and distract your baby with all the dirty vests he's created.

- Give your baby a bath. The running water and the different sensations can be very calming.
- Put your baby in a buggy and take him out for a walk or put him in the car and go for a drive.
- Be ready to jingle keys, wave a coloured handkerchief or become a yo-yo champion. I've carried many strange objects round with me to act as a distraction in awkward moments.
- Singing is another solution and you don't necessarily need to sing louder than your baby's crying. You'll be surprised how easily all the nursery rhymes you thought you'd forgotten come flooding back. Stop singing George Michael or Oasis songs in favour of Old King Cole if that's what works best; although there's always the possibility of adapting your sort of music to nursery rhyme-type actions. And you'll be amazed to discover how many times you can sing Three Blind Mice to a grumpy baby and still keep all your marbles.
- You can also try dancing. Have a look at the film *Babe* and get a few pointers from the farmer as he behaves in a totally uncharacteristic manner towards the end. Mums are driven to bizarre behaviour, believe me, in the never-ending quest to placate their babies.

If there is really nothing wrong with your baby, but he just won't settle, you may have to preserve your sanity by plonking him in his cot, making sure he's safe, and then leaving him for a bit, while you go and do something to distract yourself – whatever works for you.

I'M SO PROUD...MUM'S JUST SAID HER FIRST SWEAR WORD.

Give Me the Gripe Water, Quick!

In the early stages, colicky babies are common. You may get to the point when you think that the gripe water would do you more good than it does the baby. Babies with colic cry incessantly, usually in the evening when you're tired out, until one day they wake up and they're different children. If your baby always cries at the same time of day, try and have a break before the crying starts. Plan your day so that you're not stressed out at the same time as your baby is due to start screaming the place down. This is especially important if you're a single mum or if you have a partner who doesn't get home until after both you and the baby have crashed out in exhaustion. Don't overload yourself with things to do, concentrate on the baby. Don't try and do the hoovering, ironing and cooking at the same time. Some mums worry that they won't recognise if there's something really wrong with their child, but a sick baby either doesn't cry at all or cries more than normal or in a different way. These are the times to seek immediate medical help.

 Top Tip: Try not to overload yourself if you've got a screaming baby. Think of ways to give yourself time and space to cope.

Ruth had a baby who screamed himself sick through the first nine months of his life. It was discovered that he had a stomach problem that would sort itself out as he grew up. This was small consolation to Ruth as it meant that she had a baby who was constantly being sick or suffering from colic. Once he was upright and walking he was a different child, but until then there was little Ruth could do except comfort her unhappy son. Knowing there was a reason behind the constant screaming helped Ruth and her partner to cope and gave them a focus for their efforts.

Snakes and Ladders

Don't worry if you come to motherhood with little or no experience of babies. You're not expected to become the fount of all knowledge overnight so don't expect too much of yourself. Looking after a baby is about learning; learning about this new person in your life. As in any relationship, getting to know each other takes time, and motherhood is no exception.

Mums are traditionally expected to 'know best' but they don't know it all at once. I've been asked, many a time, what's the matter with my fractious baby and I've replied that I haven't a clue! However, it's true that the parent who spends the most time with the baby will be the one who is most tuned in to what's going on. And, as with all relationships, you can't carry over specific knowledge of one child to another. The truth is, when (and if) you have another baby you slip down a snake right back to the bottom of the game and have to work your way back up the ladders. Each child is different with a unique personality, so what you've learnt about one child doesn't automatically transfer to child number two.

Neither should you worry if you're not immediately bowled over by a gush of love for your baby. Some mums fall in love with their children the moment they lay eyes on them while others take a little longer to warm up. It doesn't mean there's something wrong with you if you don't turn to jelly at the sight of your crinkly newborn. For many mums love is part of the getting-to-know-you process. It takes time. And while some adore tiny babies, other mums find that they don't really come into their own until they've got a seven-year-old on their hands with whom they can have intelligent conversations, or a twelve-year-old they can go clothes shopping with. So don't judge yourself too harshly; no two mums are the same. And just because you're a mum doesn't mean you have to love every aspect of motherhood. How many people enjoy changing nappies for instance? Either the early days' ones filled with sticky tar or the scrambled egg explosion ones? There are jobs to be done which are neither pleasant nor fulfilling, but it all comes with the territory.

Top Tip: *Don't worry if you don't become a child expert overnight. Learning to look after a baby takes time. And remember – even the experts don't always know!*

Mums have to get used to living with contradictions: you may feel claustrophobic because you are no longer a free agent while also feeling that you can't bear to be parted from your baby. Life is a balancing act between the love you have for your child and the negativity over all the grotty jobs you have to do. And no matter how much you try you may never conquer the laundry. It can be very dissatisfying to feel that you never quite get on top of a job because the baby's needs come first, but that doesn't make you a failure.

There's no such thing as 'wash and go' – it's wash, fill nappy, wash again and get a complete change of clothes for baby, followed by puke down the back and a complete change of clothes for you, and quick . . . go!

You may long for the days when all you needed were a set of car keys and a tank full of petrol, but try and keep life in perspective. The first few months of a baby's life pass by very quickly. If you blink you'll miss them. By a month old babies have already lost their newborn look, by six months they're sitting up and may even be crawling, and once the early days are over you can't get them back so make your mind up to enjoy them as much as you can. Having a tiny baby to care for will only take up a very small amount of your life overall, although it seems all-encompassing when you're doing it.

Try and give yourself rewards to look forward to. Promise yourself treats – they needn't be expensive. A long, uninterrupted soak in the bath with a magazine is a luxury every mum should be able to arrange. Get someone else to look after the baby, such as your partner, or a good friend or relative, or failing that make the most of the times your baby falls asleep – grab a magazine and chill out for a while. I've got a friend who has a particular cup that she likes to have a cup of tea in. An odd habit maybe, but if she sits down with this particular cup she feels that she's having a break. If she's in a hurry she'll have a drink in any old cup.

Develop patterns of behaviour that *you* associate with having a break, even if they seem insignificant to everyone else. Anything which helps you to switch off for five minutes benefits the whole family. Don't neglect yourself. Give yourself time in the mornings to make yourself presentable. It's easy to slip into a pattern where all your energy is focused onto the baby and you don't allow yourself any time. If you look better, you'll feel better and more able to cope. Looking like a complete wreck does nothing for your self-image.

 Top Tip: *Remember that children grow up much quicker than you expect so make the most of every minute you spend with them.*

What They Don't Tell You In Antenatal Classes

In one episode of *Friends*, Ross comes to terms with the fact that his estranged wife is about to have their baby. The enormous responsibility suddenly dawns on him and he says, 'I always knew I was going to have a baby but I only just realised the baby was having me.' That's how a lot of parents feel. Coming to terms with looking after a baby is one thing, coming to terms with being a parent is another. It's normal to feel quite bewildered by the responsibility you acquire the moment your baby is born. Once you've got a baby you can't take it back for a better model, one that's less noisy or more economical. The responsibility can be immense.

I know many mums who have woken up in the night convinced they've lost their baby. I've often worried that I would forget I'd got a baby in tow and that I would accidentally leave it somewhere – I never did. There's an advert on the radio for French wine which captures the panic beautifully. The parents are about to toast their newborn's health when they realise that neither of them knows where the baby is. But babies aren't like car keys which you put down and can't find again half an hour later. Despite any fears you may have, you're unlikely to mislay your pride and joy. That sort of problem only becomes a possibility when you've got several children who are all out visiting friends and you can't remember who you're supposed to pick up at what time!

Responsibility for children is an awesome thing, no doubt. You may feel totally inadequate but try not to worry – most mums, and dads for that matter, feel like it from time to time. You may feel like the Ruler in the Hans Christian Andersen story who is faced with a little child shouting 'But the Emperor has nothing on at all', but it's OK to feel that you're bluffing your way along. Everybody bluffs to some extent or other, even the most experienced of mothers.

Best Supporting Actress

Being a mum means moving from centre stage when everyone is asking after you and looking after you during pregnancy, to being on the periphery. Overnight you find you're in the middle of visiting time with a host of people peering into the cot and asking about the baby's minutest detail. It's no longer you they come to see but the baby. You've suddenly acquired another role and life will never be the same again. All of us are used to playing different roles – daughter, sister, lover, friend, neighbour – so changing roles is nothing new, but when you have a baby you suddenly take on the role of mother which is so awe-inspiring that it can overshadow every other part of your life.

The transformation to mother is quicker than the transformation of a bedroom from chintz to minimalist in the TV programme *Changing Rooms*. Try to keep a balanced view and don't ignore other important members of your family. If you're on your own don't neglect friends or relatives who have supported you throughout your pregnancy; try and keep some semblance of normality going in your relationships. If you have a partner remember that he will have a lot of adjusting to do as well and he'll probably feel twice as helpless as you. Work together as you look after your baby rather than pull against each other. Share how you're feeling; the father of your baby will probably be the only one who is as involved in the day-to-day details of your baby's life.

 Top Tip: *Try not to let your role as mum take over your whole life – there are other people who need you too.*

There are some problems you can discuss together before they arise. Decide who will get up to the baby in the night before you go to bed, not at four in the morning when you're too tired to think straight. Aim to support each other as you fit into your roles as mother and father. Be practical about how you'll deal with a stream of visitors and over-enthusiastic relatives. Look further ahead and talk about how you'll nurture your baby as he grows up. Even put some thought into the less pressing details such as, for example, what names you'll use for various body parts, before you're publicly embarrassed by your two-year-old. Will you stick to anatomical descriptions, will you use something a little less formal, or will you make up your own words to describe private parts and bodily functions?

Rip Van Who?

If you have a partner, don't neglect spending time together as a couple. It's incredible how quickly you forget what it was like just to be two people instead of three. Arrange to have a romantic meal at home without junior vying for attention. Or if you have a good friend or relative who wants to go gaga over the baby, suggest they take the baby out for a twelve-mile walk on a Sunday afternoon! And then don't spend all the time you're alone talking or worrying about your baby! Talk about other things; after all, there is life outside which doesn't consist of nappy rash, teething and when to move onto baby rice.

Keep your relationship with your partner at the centre of your family; don't allow the mother/child relationship to overshadow what should be the pivot on which the whole family moves. Make time for each other and appreciate each other. Move the baby's cot to another room for an evening if that's what it takes to find time together. And make the most of every opportunity to be alone together, for however short a time. Time together as a couple is at a premium when you have a baby. And the situation doesn't improve as children get older. By the time your child is sixteen, you won't have any evenings alone together as he'll be going to bed later than you.

Make sure you don't end up like Rip Van Winkle, who went to sleep in an enchanted place one night and woke the following morning to discover that twenty years had passed. In the same way that your baby grows, your relationship with your partner needs to grow. You don't want to wake up one morning and discover your partner has become a complete stranger. So get into a good habit right from the beginning by actively creating time for the two of you when you're not too exhausted to enjoy it. Put the nappies in a pile in the corner and ignore them for a while.

No Straitjacket Required

How Do I Deal with Tantrums, Telltales and Trouble?

The word compliance is defined in the Collins dictionary as a 'disposition to yield or comply with others'. Our eldest son Benjamin, when he was coming up for two years old, was not compliant. He used to have the most awful temper tantrums: he would lie on the ground and kick and scream for what seemed like hours on end. To make matters worse it was guaranteed to happen at 3 o'clock every day when I was standing in the school playground waiting for the older children. There was absolutely nothing I could do with this flailing two-year-old except ignore him as he lay on the ground and thrashed about. His yells echoed my embarrassment around the playground and I felt that I was living proof that useless mums exist. When my two daughters came out of school I had to wedge Benjamin, still screaming, under my arm and carry him to the car, while pushing a baby in a buggy and trying to take in all the information my daughters were bending my ears with. Then I was faced with the prospect of strapping him into his car seat, an event that could take anything up to fifteen minutes. I looked and felt like a harassed mother: I wanted to scream at the world to stop so I could get off; I wanted to stick a paper bag over my head and pretend it wasn't happening to me; I wanted the school playground to open up and swallow me, screaming toddler and all.

Temper tantrums are a terrible drain on a mum's confidence. They have several causes: tiredness, frustration or attention-seeking. If your child has one at home, it's not so difficult to make sure she can't hurt herself and then let her get on with it, but when a toddler has one in the middle of a public place it's a different problem. Threats and enticements are useless weapons in the face of raging toddlers: they will throw sweets and drinks through the air with the skill of David against Goliath. Someone once said that you could take over the world with an army of two-year-olds. And anyone who's ever seen a two-year-old in full flood will find that easy to believe.

- Make sure your toddler has enough sleep, then she'll be less likely to get irritable and bad-tempered.
- Do your best to ignore your toddler when she's having a tantrum. If she's attention-seeking she'll settle for any attention – even if it's your glaring eyes and cross words.
- Stay as calm as possible.
- Try and give your toddler time to do things, such as examining all the insects on garden walls on the way to the shops

or the park, instead of always rushing. Less pressure = less frustration.

- Remember that small children don't understand the concept of time passing so they find it difficult to wait. Use waiting time as an opportunity to talk to your toddler rather than ignoring her and letting her frustration build up.

- Teach your child about sharing and the fact that some things can't be shared. Babies are naturally selfish up to the age of about two and a half and will want someone else's toy even if they've got a roomful to play with. The more you teach them about what they can and can't share, the fewer tantrums they're likely to have in the long term.

- Don't allow temper tantrums to take over your whole life. Focus on good behaviour and praise your toddler when she does something good. Praise her especially when she shows self-control and stops having a tantrum.

- You may feel as if the whole world is looking at you and judging you but in reality most people will be sympathising.

 Top Tip: *Your best defence in the face of a toddler's rage is calmness.*

When we got home after Benjamin's outbursts I would sit and cuddle my red-faced, sweaty son and often he'd fall asleep in my arms. It was the only way I could express that I loved him, despite his appalling behaviour. During that period of about eighteen months I was at my wits' end and felt like a complete failure. Benjamin slowly grew out of tantrums and grew into a happy, even-tempered boy. There was nothing I could do to prevent his behaviour, as we had to go to school each day whether he liked it or not; all I could do was love him, and show him I loved him, through it.

What Can I Do to Stop You Loving Me?

Sometimes it's easy to love your child. You get that warm gushy feeling and motherhood seems a breeze. You smile lovingly at your infant and wonder how you could have ever felt stressed out. Showing children love is easy when they're behaving like cherubs but when they're throwing tantrums or being plain disobedient it's a different matter. All of us need to know we're loved, warts and all. We don't want to be loved only when we're happy and smiling, we want to be loved when we've got a streaming cold and have just burnt the toast. And we never grow out of that need to be accepted in spite of our short-comings.

Learning to show that you love your child when she's being uncooperative is like learning a difficult piece of piano music. It takes hours of repetitive hard work. Most children go through difficult phases but the wonderful thing is that they generally come out the other side, noticing only that their mother has more grey hair and a look of relief on her face. There are many times when children will test your love to the limits, and often what they're really doing is stretching you to see just how far your love goes. Will you love me even if . . . ? So it's important to show them you love them, even if . . . And that might mean cuddling a stroppy child or spending time giving a two-year-old and his drawing your undivided attention when you're at the tricky part of a recipe. The kind of love that says 'I love you no matter what you do or what I'm doing' gives security, and children need to feel secure in their parents' love. A child's greatest fear is not that burglars will break into the house when he's asleep or that his parents will divorce but that he will be abandoned.

 Top Tip: *Your son or daughter needs to know you love them not only when they're being good but also when they've had a temper tantrum or behaved badly.*

Telltale Tit

Louise has a daughter who tells tales, all the time. Lucy constantly tries to get her little brother into trouble. The problem is that occasionally it's useful to know what he's up to but most of the time it's just plain annoying. Louise hit upon a solution. She bought a book of raffle tickets, the sort you get in stationers, and every day she gives Lucy three tickets. Lucy is allowed to tell three tales a day but no more, so every time she goes running to her mother with another piece of juicy information she must give in one of her tickets. Invariably Lucy is not so keen to rush off to her mum with tittle-tattle as she's frightened she'll use up all her tickets and miss the best opportunity of the day to tell a really good tale. She often goes to bed with a ticket or two in hand, which is not carried over!

Don't telltales drive you nuts! They give you pieces of information that, generally speaking, you would rather not know about. I sometimes use the tactic with tale-telling as well as with bickering that if the children can't say something nice then they shouldn't say anything at all. This approach is normally worth about one minute of utter silence. It's a fact of life that children do things they shouldn't, but as a mum you're trying to create a loving, stable environment not a Boot Camp. Children have a very strong sense of justice and they equate fairness with being right and unfairness with being wrong. The problem, of course, is that life is not fair. Sooner or later they will have to learn the fact that no matter how good they are, life will not always be a bowl of strawberry ice cream.

- Explain to your child that you intend to be fair but it may not always appear like that to her. Gently help her come to terms with the idea that the world is sometimes an unfair place.
- Teach your child discretion – not every mistake needs to be put right. Some misdemeanours are too minor to worry about. Explain that you don't really need to know that your other two children have been calling each other 'Poo Face' before amicably settling down in front of the TV together.
- Some mistakes get righted while the tale is being told and before you have a chance to shout and scream – you can't tell a child off when she's frantically mopping up an accidentally spilt drink. You might prefer to encourage her to be more careful before helping her finish the job.
- Remember that by putting someone else down your child feels she is automatically raising herself up. It's a case of 'Hey, look at me, I'm the good guy', so don't reinforce the fact that snitching on someone is good. Let your child know that telling tales is as unacceptable as getting the goldfish out of the bowl to see how it's doing.
- Try to recognise that telling tales is an attention-seeking device like tantrums.
- Find practical solutions to difficulties, where they exist. If there are no obvious solutions, don't tear your hair out by the handful; instead keep going and look for any flicker of light that might be the end of the tunnel.

Top Tip: *Do your best to show your child you love her, by talking and listening to her, however badly she's behaved.*

Here Comes Trouble

Sharon is going through a difficult patch with one of her children. Her daughter Anna seems to demand constant attention. Even with the best will in the world it is something which no mother can give. It doesn't seem to matter how many bedtime stories Sharon reads to Anna, or how much she does with her on a one-to-one basis, Anna is always demanding something more. Sharon finds it very frustrating when her daughter interrupts her in the middle of something, so she's set out boundaries of when Anna can and cannot interrupt her. It means both have to keep their side of the bargain and Sharon has to be willing sometimes to stop what she's doing to make time for her daughter.

Children don't always appreciate just how difficult their behaviour can be. Most of the time they don't realise that they're doing something annoying and frustrating. Our children have a horrible habit of turning the television volume to high as soon as they switch it on. It drives me mad. I could really do with a tape recording which hollers at them several times 'Turn it down!' Minor things can get lumped together with bigger problems. When you're telling them off for coming home late it may be tempting to throw in the bit about having the radio on too loud the day before yesterday. But it's important to deal with each problem on its own rather than treat it as part of a campaign against your standards. Work with your partner, if you have one, or a trusted friend in solving problems – don't try and work it all out on your own even if you spend more time with your child than anyone else. Remember:

- **Keep the lines of communication open,** no matter what your child has done. And when you do talk, make eye contact. There's nothing more unsettling than trying to hold a conversation with someone who won't make eye contact with you. Eye contact affirms whoever you're talking to; it gives them value. It also shows them that you're paying attention to what they're saying and not listening with one ear tuned to the radio.
- **Don't be tempted to resort to Cold War tactics.** When your child has done something wrong she needs to know. My friend Ann had a mother who frequently used silence as a punishment. On one occasion Ann's mother didn't speak to her for several days without ever telling her daughter what she had done wrong. Ann was expected to guess what the problem was throughout three isolating, miserable days. And she never did. In the end, Ann's mother told her why she wouldn't talk to her – the reason being little more than a misunderstanding.
- **Don't struggle on your own.** Ask for help if you need it and try not to equate the need for help with failure. The people who fail are the ones who don't recognise that they are facing a problem. Once you start talking you're on the way to finding a solution. So overcome the hurdle and talk to friends, family or anyone whose opinion you value.

Top Tip: *Asking for help does not mean you're a failure.*

Stress levels vary during the day. Mums find the most stressful times with their children are getting them off to school in the morning and putting them to bed at night. Try not to overstretch yourself at a time that you know is particularly stressful for you. I've been known, in a mad moment, to start hoovering as well as clearing all the breakfast things up in the few remaining minutes before we go out. I can feel the tension rising in me as I take on far too much, and then I wonder why the children are peering at me rather strangely round half-closed doors.

Give yourself as much time as you can when going out or when you're putting your child to bed. Frantically bundling your five-year-old into bed while trying to get ready for an evening out is destined for failure. Children need time to unwind at the end of the day, just as much as you do, so try and build some relaxation time before the bedtime routine – it'll do both of you good!

'The Man Who Makes No Mistakes Does Not Usually Make Anything'

As a family we muddle along, making numerous mistakes as we go. Learning to forgive your children for their misdemeanours is one thing, teaching them to forgive you for yours is another. And when we get it wrong, or explode in the heat of the moment, it's our turn to say sorry. If you've been really angry with your child before she goes to school it's important to sort it out before she leaves you for six hours. And it's you, the mum, who needs to make the effort to overcome simmering anger and resentment, to explain how you're feeling and be the first to apologise.

Most of us feel horribly guilty when we've been angry with a child and doled out a punishment that didn't fit the crime. This usually happens when we're tired and another bout of misbehaviour or squabbling becomes the final straw. That's the point to stop, take stock and go and speak to the child you've sent to her room. It's also the point to recognise your own failings. Done in honesty and openness, children are quick to respond and learn by example.

 Top Tip: *The best way to teach children forgiveness is by forgiving them.*

Forgiving isn't always easy. It may take effort but it's the only way to move on. Sometimes, in retrospect, our mistakes can take on legendary proportions. My children take great delight in reminding me about some of the disastrous mistakes I've made. A few years ago we were on holiday in Norfolk during a bitterly cold April when a particularly infamous walk took place. And, as with all legends, it's a story that has become more elaborate with every telling.

I had managed to persuade the rest of the family that a bird-watching walk on the marshes by the sea was just the thing we

49

all needed. We had with us a large assortment of ill-fitting hats and mismatched gloves, so everyone was duly wrapped up before we set off. The wind was, shall we say, 'bracing' and the ground was muddy. We had walked quite a way along the coastal path when the children's grumbles changed. They began to argue about the snow, or was it hail, or was it frozen peas that they could see heading towards us. I was about to tell them that it couldn't possibly be any of those when I looked across the marshes and saw a hail storm heading our way. By this time we were past the point of no return on our gentle walk. The nearest shelter of any kind was about a mile away, the car was about two miles in the opposite direction. We had a family conference and decided the best plan was to head for shelter from the impending storm and worry about getting back to the car later.

After ten minutes we were in the middle of the storm which was a mixture of hail, sleet and snow. I took to singing 'The Wheels on the Bus Go Round', in a vain attempt to keep everyone moving. The wheels on the pushchair hardly went round at all in the sludge as we ploughed on with grim determination. Feet were cold, hands were frozen and I didn't have enough tissues for all the tear-stained faces and runny noses. Finally, we stumbled onto the hard tarmac of the road and squelched our way into a tearoom. It would have been nice to end the story there, but by this time we were still over a mile and a half from the car, towards which, after a long pause for refreshments and toe-warming, we headed off.

The children, from the largest to the smallest, were furious with Mike and I for having made them walk six miles in such terrible weather. And who could blame them? We drove back to the house with accusations ringing in our ears and as the children thawed out and warmed up their tempers warmed up too. Our apologies at first fell on deaf ears, and they were more intent on venting their anger than listening to us lamely explain that we'd made a big mistake. I was singled out as particularly to blame as it was all my idea in the first place. Eventually all the children accepted our apologies with a promise that we would never do that walk again. We were forgiven and family harmony was restored – at least for a while.

 Top Tip: Don't forget to forgive yourself when you get it wrong.

It can be hard for a child to accept that her mum is anything less than perfect. We all hear playground stories of the child who boasts how wonderful her mother is and if we're honest we'd like our children to think of us as a Supermum. But we're not Supermum, we're fallible: if only we could jump into a phone box and come out as a different person, complete with satin cape and a solution to every problem. The first step in teaching your child to forgive you is to forgive yourself for getting it wrong. You should aim to be like the ice skaters who stumble and fall, then get up and, without faltering for a moment, go on to perform a triple salchow with a perfect landing.

• Don't get hung up about mistakes; learn from what you've done wrong then put the past behind you.

51

- Be ready to make the first move and say sorry. As well as being a step towards peace it's also a good example.
- Look for ways to compromise in difficult situations.
- Don't add a burden of guilt, to you or your children, every time you or they muck things up. Deal with problems and then forget them.
- Keep a sense of perspective. A big issue today may simply go away of its own accord in a couple of weeks. And children do grow up – eventually.

Bogey Men under the Bed

How Do I Stop Worrying about My Child?

I was at my friend Sarah's house for what should have been a relaxed morning of coffee and chat. I had with me my two-year-old son who was a walking (or rather toddling) tornado. He was at that point in life where everything was of great interest and had to be investigated. So there we were, having a quiet cup of coffee, when, for just a second, he toddled out of sight.

A moment later there was the crash of a door slamming. I leapt up, coffee splashing, and rushed to see what had happened. At first it appeared that my small tornado had simply shut the door behind him as he went into Sarah's lounge, then we realised that the door handle had fallen off (she'd been meaning to get it fixed for a while) and was in the lounge with him. All that was left was the sticking out square bit of metal that was balanced precariously through the lock.

I could hear a bash and a burble through the thick wooden

door, then silence. I began to panic. The windows were tightly shut and double glazed, but far worse than both of these was the fact that Sarah had been ironing in the room just before I arrived and the iron, although switched off, was still hot. I could feel the fear rising, but I managed to keep it under control. As I shut my mouth tightly I felt terror creep round the back of my head and appear in my eyes. We needed either a screwdriver or a fireman; we opted for the former first of all.

Sarah disappeared into the cupboard under the stairs for what seemed at least three weeks while I stood, trying to make reassuring noises to a little boy who had got bored with this game and wanted to go home. I consoled myself with the thought that while he was crying he couldn't be climbing up the curtains – I knew he found it hard to do both at the same time. All the while, visions of the Fire Brigade breaking in through the double glazed windows and other images too terrible to mention sped through my mind.

Finally, after a lot of rummaging and clattering in the cupboard, Sarah emerged with a big smile on her face. I turned from my vigil to see her holding a light bulb triumphantly in the air. The fear finally burst free from where it was hiding and I started to yell at her. How did she think we were going to break into a locked room armed with a light bulb? It turned out that there was no light in the cupboard, so in order to look for a screwdriver, a light bulb had to be found. I could only make high-pitched squeaking noises as Sarah disappeared back into the cupboard. A moment later a light came on and soon we were busy removing another door handle and fixing it to her lounge door.

At last a small, tearful boy was reunited with his equally

tearful mother. I declined the offer of a cup of tea to steady my nerves, preferring to get to the relative safety of my own home, where I knew that the door handles were tightly fixed and there was a light in the cupboard under the stairs.

Fight or Flight?

Fear is a strange thing. The sudden surge of adrenaline enables you to react – it's known as the fight-or-flight mechanism. You're ready either to face your enemy or to run like a hundred-metre sprinter. You're ready to act in a split second, to reach out and grab the toddler as he runs into the road or shout at the five-year-old as she rides her bike into the path of her nine-year-old brother on the swing. And there are many times when you need that quick reaction. But too much adrenaline can work against you too. If you're in a situation where you feel you can do nothing, you can end up either squeaking incoherently or running round like the proverbial headless chicken. The problems start when that surge of panic comes too frequently; at times when there really is no need to either run or fight. The adrenaline just whizzes round your body looking for something useful to do. The answer is to try and avoid unnecessary panic, which sends your body into a state. Remember that worry will not add a single hour to your life – in fact it will most probably take hours off! Neither will worry sort out your problem for you. Turn your efforts instead to things you *can* do to alleviate the situation.

Top Tip: *Worry without action achieves nothing of any good so try not to worry unnecessarily.*

Fear needn't be quite so dramatic though. It can run at a lower level through our lives as we worry about our children, their safety, their future or the problems that they are having at school. We create fear out of what might be, not what is. We worry about what will become of our children; we worry about whether they'll pass exams, get a job, or cope in a world that gets more pressurised by the day. It has only been in the last century that we've been given the luxury of worrying about what our children will achieve; the biggest worry used to be whether or not children would survive, not whether they'd pass their GCSEs in sixteen years' time.

However common it may be, worry is still neither useful nor productive. On its own it's a powerless monster which shouts 'boo' and makes you jump but really does not have any power to hurt you. Most of our worries are unwarranted and, as such, should be relegated to comic strips where they can boo and growl to their heart's delight.

When Will I See You Again?

Alison has a ten-year-old son who doesn't like going away from home very much. He's a well-balanced child but simply prefers the security of his own environment. Alison really started worrying when she found out, six months before the event,

56

MORE AND MORE PARENTS ARE REALISING I'M USELESS... AND THAT **SCARES** ME.

that the school had planned a residential field trip which meant Jack would have to stay away from home for a few nights. True to form Jack announced that he didn't want to go on the trip and that was that. Over the next few months, however, it became clear that everyone else in Jack's class was going and he was the only one who had refused. Alison was torn between not wanting to pressurise her son into something he was clearly uncomfortable about and not wanting him to be the only one to miss out on a good time with the rest of his class mates. Alison took the decision to lay off the pressure and instead to accentuate the positive side of the trip. She was delighted when, a week or so before the class disappeared into the big wide world, Jack changed his mind and signed up.

The week that Jack was away was hell for Alison. Having been stressed about the situation for six months it had become such a problem in her mind that she couldn't just switch off. When Jack arrived back home, however, Alison couldn't believe the difference. While she had spent a week fretting, Jack had been having a whale of a time, so much so that he declared he hadn't missed any of his family and it was a pity he was back!

Can't Sleep, Won't Sleep

Sleepless nights do no one any good, but it's very hard to switch off from what may seem insurmountable problems. The most important thing is to recognise what you can sort out and what you can't – as the prayer goes, 'Give me the serenity to accept the things I cannot change, the courage to change the things I can and the wisdom to know the difference.' Knowing what you can sort out and what you simply have to leave is vital to keeping peace of mind.

 Top Tip: *Learn to relax so you don't spend endless hours lying awake and fretting.*

For example, if your child is having a problem either at home or at school, find someone you can talk to. A good place to start is with a friend or someone else you can trust. Make sure it's not another mum who has already won the award of 'Champion Worrier' and who will just wind you up even more.

It's amazing how many burdens we carry, believing we're the only one to have such problems. When you start talking to other mums you often find that lots of children won't eat properly and prefer to live on biscuits and sweets and you're not the only one to be worried about your child's development. Developmental milestones are there only as a guide so don't panic if your child doesn't rigidly adhere to them. Most children are far more resilient than we give them credit for. Do not be unduly worried about the fact that your child collects snails, gives them names (which he writes on their shells) and puts them in the bathroom. And don't get too carried away worrying about the unlikely; the fact that your son or daughter dismembers Barbie dolls does not necessarily mean they will end up as a serial killer.

It's when you start talking to other mums at pre-school group or in the playground that you realise you're not the only parent in the world to have discipline problems with a two-year-old who insists on posting crisps and pencils into the video recorder. Children may not all do the same things, but they all go through the same stages. Reassurance from other mums can come as a wonderful relief.

Top Tip: *Talk to other mums and discover you're not the only one in the world with a stroppy child!*

Lights, Camera . . . Action!

If problems are more serious, then you need to take action. If you're worried sick about your child at school, make an appointment to see your child's teacher rather than spend sleepless nights convinced there is no solution. Take positive action rather than fretting. To say 'I must do something' is far better than saying 'Something must be done'. If your child is ill and you're concerned, take him to see a doctor rather than spend an hour reading up on every conceivable illness in the medical book and imagining the worst. Doctors are well practised at reassuring over-anxious mums and as long as you don't call them out in the middle of the night with something as minor as a spot on the nose, they're happy to put your mind at rest. Health visitors, pharmacists and other health-care professionals are there to help you, so go and see them and make the most of their knowledge.

In *Winnie-the-Pooh* there's a chapter entitled 'In which Pooh and Piglet go hunting and nearly catch a Woozle'. It's a wonderful story whereby Pooh and Piglet mistake their own footprints in the snow for those of some strange creature. The more they wander round in circles getting increasingly anxious about 'whatever-it-is', the more footprints they create. And the more footprints they see, the more worried they become in case the strange creatures are of 'Hostile Intent'.

There's a fine line between the worry that goes round in aimless circles when nothing is really wrong and the nagging doubt in your mind that drives you into some sort of action. Weigh up exactly what is worrying you and work out which category it falls into. Often the very fact that you're doing something practical such as speaking to a teacher or doctor or another mum is enough to take the edge off the fear.

I have the problem that I suffer with a chronic illness. This means that I am often unwell and spend my whole life walking a tightrope of health. Not only have I worried about the state my body is in but also the effect that the trips to the hospital and frequent days in bed have on the children. When I'm unwell, my options are limited and if I want to avoid hospitalisation I have to stay in bed. I used to worry about the fact that I wasn't a 'normal' mother because 'normal' mothers didn't have to lie down at seven o'clock every evening; neither did they sit on the kitchen floor and cry when they didn't feel very well. Over a period of time, however, I've noticed that on the days I have to lie down, the children come and sit and talk to me. They rarely squabble around the bed and generally take it in turns either to chat about their day or to bring some homework or reading to do with me. The TV may be on downstairs but upstairs I'm a captive audience, free from distractions, and as long as they don't bounce all over me like chimpanzees I'll listen. It's been amazing to see how the very thing that worried me has ended up turning into something good.

Curtain Twitching

There comes a time with older children when they are old enough to be out and about on their own and you simply have to trust that they'll be safe. Short of following teenagers around and escorting them across the road, or using some sort of global positioning device which tracks their every movement, there's little you can do to ensure their safe return and worrying does absolutely nothing to help. Obviously, if they're late home, it may be time to take action. The trick again is learning when it's OK to be concerned and when you're fretting unnecessarily.

Our daughters usually arrive home from school at pretty much the same time every day. I know, however, that sometimes the buses are late or full or non-existent, so I have a built-in half an hour or so of leeway time that should cover all possibilities. After that if they're not home or haven't rung, I usually end up twitching curtains at regular intervals and battling to stop my mind running riot. Invariably they saunter through the door and ask me what's wrong. I know this does me no good whatsoever but I'm working on it, ever hopeful that I will one day be awash with serenity instead.

Top Tip: *Try to recognise which worries need to be sorted out and which will resolve themselves given time.*

'Leave Your Worry on the Doorstep'

Our children have a video game where the aim is to collect seven crying babies and save them from the nasty big blue alien blobs. The babies all crawl along happily behind the hero as he vaporises the threatening aliens. It's one game that I have no desire to play – there's too much truth in it for me as a mum! When you're stressed out with worry over your children you may end up feeling as if you've got to protect them from 'whatever is out there'. Whether or not you have seven babies to placate, don't worry yourself into believing that the world is plagued with enormous blue alien blobs – creatures that are just out to get you.

If you're already a champion worrier, find things to do to occupy your time and take your mind off all those possibilities you can't change. Do something *you* want to do, or failing that, do something you've been putting off, like tidying the cupboard under the stairs or cleaning the oven. It's amazing how physical activity can be a tonic for the mind. Make a conscious effort to stop the worry before it gets a grip. Don't get in a tizz about whether or not your child will settle into school six months before he starts. Cross each bridge when you get to it and not three years beforehand – a lot can happen in the intervening time and you may find the bridge has moved. Unfortunately, we can't look into the future and see what it will bring so that we can sort out problems ahead of schedule. The only thing you can do is to prepare your child for what lies ahead, to the best of your ability. Ensure his safety as far as it's within your power to do so, then let him get on with it. The vast majority of children reach adulthood safely, pass exams and find jobs regardless of how much their mothers worry. They do not do better if you panic more!

- Free-floating worry does no one any good. It actually achieves nothing positive at all. You can spend your life worrying about something which may never happen. Don't let your mind run away with you – keep it in check.
- Enjoy what you have today rather than always fretting

about what you may not have tomorrow.

- Don't build up the part. Don't blow up minor problems out of all proportion just so that you've got something really serious to worry about.

 Top Tip: Keeping things in perspective will help your sanity.

Like Mother Like Daughter, Like Father Like Son?

'All women become like their mothers.' The famous quotation from Oscar Wilde's play *The Importance of Being Earnest* is enough to give many mums apoplexy! For some women, the fear that they are turning into their mothers is a nightmare. If you have had a bad experience of mothering you may worry about repeating the endless cycle, unable to break out of a pre-formed rut. Some mums look for any little sign that this metamorphosis is taking place – they peer strangely into the mirror to see if their mum is peering back – while others simply give in to what they believe is the inevitable.

In the *Star Wars* films, Darth Vader believes that Luke Skywalker, his son, is destined to follow in his footsteps and become evil. To make sure this happens Darth Vader traps his son and hands him over to the evil Emperor. Luke has other ideas and manages to escape. Not only does he succeed in breaking the cycle but Luke also believes that his father has the capacity to change back from evil to good. It's not enough that he was not prepared to complete the cycle but he's determined to do all he can to put the whole thing into reverse.

The truth is that no one is exactly like their mother, or father for that matter, and all of us are able to develop and learn from the successes and mistakes of the past. So don't accept what you feel is inevitable. You need to develop an identity that is separate from your own mother. Think about your mum's positive aspects, her abilities and the values you respect. Consider what you feel was wrong with your upbringing and look at practical ways whereby you can avoid making the same mistakes. If you need to, forgive your mother – in your heart if not actually in person – for the things she got wrong, and move on. Don't be tied by what has gone before.

We all bring images of how to be a mum to motherhood. This may be an *Absolutely Fabulous* image based on what our mother was like or a stereotype based on all the things our mother was not. True, our mothers (and grandmothers) will have a significant effect on our ideals but remember that you will develop a style of parenting which is entirely your own.

Contrary to popular belief, life *is* in fact pretty much a bed of roses – thorns as well as flowers. Whether you concentrate on the thorns or the roses helps to determine how happy you'll be. There are few moments in life when there is nothing to worry about; few days when children behave impeccably and there are no traumas about to press their ugly faces against the window. When those moments appear make the most of them because they're precious. Soak them up and don't search for something to worry about. And at the end of the day, remember most of those nitty-gritty things that spend hours consuming you will be resolved in time, and you'll forget the majority of them ever happened!

PART TWO: PRACTICALITIES

'For My Next Trick'

How Do I Juggle Work and Family?

In the film *Multiplicity* the main character, Doug, believes that having several copies of himself will make his life easier. He decides to experiment in cloning, and before long there are four Dougs, all suited to the various aspects of Doug's life. One is an expert in housework and looking after the children; one takes his place at work; one turns out to be completely useless and sits in the garage eating, which leaves the original Doug with time on his hands to do whatever he chooses. To begin with it all goes well and each clone is able to cover for the other when there's a problem, but eventually the characters get into a muddle. In the end, life becomes far more complicated for Doug than it was when there was just one of him and he discovers that even when you've got four bodies life is extremely hard!

Mums have always worked outside the home; it's not a new phenomenon. Mums have been working for hundreds of years. A census taken in 1901 showed that there were four million working women in England and Wales. And while we all have images of Victorian upper-class ladies doing nothing but sewing and swishing around a big house in enormous skirts, the truth is that most women were working class and many worked in appalling conditions. Women had babies and then went back to work, often working a much longer day than we do and spending far less time with their children than we expect to now. It was only as the century progressed that the idea of stay-at-home mothers came to the fore, with the 'good' mother being equated with the one who spent all her time homemaking. Now it's full circle and we're back to a situation where it's recognised that many mums have to work. A juggling act comes with the territory of motherhood and, let's face it, when you've a new baby you need all the money you can get.

What's changed is that while mums accept that they may have to work, or want to work, they often feel as if they're failing their offspring by not being at home. Guilt is not always a bad thing; sometimes it's what you need to prod you into action and make you sort out a problem. But feeling guilty because you're never where you want to be and because you can't live up to your own standards is a Catch 22. We now know so much about our children's development that we don't just have crises about their health, we have crises about their psychological make-up as well.

Knowledge is a double-edged sword and the only way to handle it is to accept the situation you're in and aim to get the best from it. Be honest with yourself about the choices you've made and why you've made them. If you've chosen to work you can concentrate on the benefits you're bringing to the whole family, so take a positive view of what you're doing. As long as you make sure that work doesn't take over your whole life and the children get pushed to the bottom of the pile, go for it. Whatever your circumstances you will constantly have to re-evaluate your priorities and commitments to keep pace with your child. Keep in mind, though, that children grow up very quickly and there's only a small window of opportunity to spend time with them.

 Top Tip: *Be honest with yourself. If you're feeling guilty about the way you juggle work and family, stop and take stock. If the guilt is justified, act on it – if it's not, don't dwell on it.*

Linda has two school-age children and works in a hospital. Although Linda's husband Tom has a reasonable income, they cannot manage on his salary alone. The biggest problem that Linda wrestles with is not the issue of child care, as they've found a wonderful child minder, but the guilt she feels about not being there for her children. Linda feels that she's failing her children by going out to work but equally feels she'd be failing them if she stayed at home and was unable to provide for them financially. It doesn't matter what she does, she's caught in a guilt trap.

Guilt seems to be part of the job description for so many working mums. If you're feeling guilty because you go out to work don't lose sight of the fact that by working you're providing for your children: by working, you're putting food on their plates and shoes on their feet. Be realistic in your expectations. In an ideal world you might have chosen to do things differently: in an ideal world mums would get paid £300,000 a year for everything they do (so the chap on the radio tells me), but unfortunately the world we inhabit is far from ideal. Neither should you hit yourself over the head by making comparisons to your childhood. Many mums today had mothers who didn't go out to work. Your mother's generation might have done it differently but that doesn't mean you have to do the same. Define your own role by the way you handle work and children in tandem rather than viewing them as two creatures locked in mortal combat.

Of course, there are some mums who go to the other extreme. Angela has three children and works, near home, in an office. The company she works for provides a crèche so she takes her youngest daughter with her. The two older children are at school and in order to get them there she pays for a taxi to take them every day; she also arranges for someone to pick them up from school and give the children tea. On top of all this Angela pays for help with the washing and ironing. Angela's work colleagues think she's nuts as it's obvious to them that she can't really cope with the situation. What's more they think she doesn't need to because guess what? At the end of the day she makes no money at all. Her salary barely covers the cost of all her child-care/housework arrangements. Angela works because she loves her job and can't bear not to be there. The question that begs to be asked is whether or not the stress of all this expensive juggling is worth it. My own point of view is that I suspect not. Working and raising a family is a balancing act on a tightrope of everybody's needs, not just Mum's.

 Top Tip: *You might feel that you're not living up to your ideals as a mum but remember that by working you're providing for your family.*

Pick Any One from Three

Work after having a child falls into three categories: either you'll go back to your job once you've had maternity leave and carry on as before, only more tired; or you'll give up your current job and work part-time (part-time jobs are invariably less well paid but you may find you can earn enough to make ends meet); or you'll work from home. If you're a zoo-keeper the last option may not be open to you but if you've got computer skills, for example, it's a possibility. There are pros and cons in all categories and because society tends to value work over motherhood, making it all fit together will be down to you and your ingenuity. By continuing in your original job you'll have to do a lot of juggling but you will maintain your career progression. If you work part-time, you may have to settle for doing something less rewarding but you won't have to worry about child care every day.

Working from home gives you the opportunity to look after your child yourself but that too has its own frustrations. As I sit trying to write I'm constantly under fire from all sorts of strange questions which I answer at best badly, and at worst not at all, because I'm totally preoccupied with what I'm doing. I do not have oodles of time to sit and write – my day is broken up in segments which fit around all the fetching and carrying I'm expected to do. I'm told at 8 o'clock in the morning that one of my children must have a new PE bag tomorrow or else; another joins in with 'While you're out shopping can you get me a new fountain pen/folder for school/French dictionary because I've lost mine/present for Hailey's party tonight, etc.', and suddenly I see my five hours of designated work time evaporating in front of my very eyes. And in the school holidays it's worse. All four children dragged a climbing frame up the garden so they could get onto a flat roof while I was sitting by the window working on the computer – I looked over my shoulder just in time. And if you've got a small child, the demands may be different but the frustrations are exactly the same. If I don't do all these jobs I feel guilty; if I do them I feel frustrated. It's a no-win situation. The answer is to make sure I'm not overrun with unreasonable demands and only do what is essential; the rest of the jobs can wait for a designated 'running-round-chasing-my-tail day' – no more than one of those a week please.

 Top Tip: *Try not to allow yourself to get overrun with unreasonable demands at work or at home.*

I Want Someone to Care

The best you can do for a child when you're working is to make sure that she has good quality care from people you trust. Find out what provisions are made for child care in your area – facilities vary greatly. Your local council will have a list of registered child-minders. Always take up references and trust your own judgment; you know what kind of environment will suit your child best so if you've got any doubts find someone else. Ask other mums who they would recommend – the grapevine is a useful source of information, the sort of information that you may not find on official lists. Your child will need some time to get to know the person who's going to care for her, so arrange a couple of afternoons before you disappear into the big blue yonder to see how they get on together. If you're able to afford a nanny – and bear in mind that nannies can cost as much as buying a new car every year – you won't have so many problems when it comes to school holidays and teacher-training days (which spring up, sometimes without warning). Nannies come in all shapes and sizes and they needn't be female and look like Mary Poppins. You may not find one who is 'practically perfect in every way' but the important thing to note when you walk through the front door at the end of a busy day is whether or not your child seems happy and well looked after.

There are more and more private nurseries springing up, which again vary in provision and cost. Go and have a look at several in order to find the one you're happiest with. The higher the proportion of carers to children, the more individual attention your child will receive. Your child will spend a great deal of time there so make sure there's plenty to keep her occupied. Finding good child care is not just about finding somewhere that's safe, it's also about finding surroundings where your child will be encouraged in her development. So don't be afraid to ask questions:

- Will she be confined to one room all the time?
- Is there somewhere she can play outside in good weather?
- Do the children ever go out on trips to places such as the local library?

Children who are well looked after thrive and while every child needs her mother, she does not need her all the time. As a child gets older it becomes increasingly obvious that you alone are unable to be all things to her. Children need other adults so they can learn how to interact. Imagine what your child would turn out like if you were around her every minute of the day – she'd never learn that mums have lives of their own.

Moving on to Plan Z

It's often said that the best laid plans fall apart and this can be especially true of child care. Unforeseen events and illnesses can crop up, so try always to have a back-up. What's more, make sure you've got back-ups to your back-ups so that if you've opted for a child-minder and she goes sick you've got other people you can call on to look after your child.

 Top Tip: *You can never have too many back-up plans, so make as many as possible.*

If you're working, think about how you're going to cope before your child gets ill. There's nothing worse than finding yourself in blind panic at seven o'clock in the morning while mopping up a bed full of last night's regurgitated dinner and trying to think up an emergency plan at the same time. Most employers will let you have time off in an emergency, though it may have to be taken as unpaid leave. You may be fortunate enough to have grandparents or other relatives living close enough to help you out. If not, you'll have to rely on trusted friends who are flexible enough not to mind a phone call at 7.30 a.m.!

Friends of mine say to me that they sometimes feel that children have a limited supply of love to give, so that if the child-minder uses it all up there will be nothing left over for them – it's not true! As mum you'll be the main focus of your child's love whether you work or not. If you have problems with a child who doesn't want to be parted from you in the mornings, create some time so that you can start a project together which you'll finish later. Maybe read the beginning of a book together with the promise that you'll finish it when you get home. Anything that builds continuity into your lives will help your child. Do something that she will look forward to completing on your return. It will also help to fix in her mind the idea that you will be coming back. Usually a few minutes spent listening outside the front door will be enough to reassure you that, once over the initial parting, your child quickly settles down. If you're still worried, ring during the day and find out how she is. Take steps to reassure yourself rather than fret all day. When you're at work try to concentrate on what you're doing and give it your best effort. Equally, when you're at home do the same. Avoid spending your life always feeling bad about what you'd rather/ought to be doing.

Good Housekeeping

One old encyclopaedia describes housekeeping as 'one of the most comprehensive occupations that a woman can undertake'. Back in the 1950s women were encouraged to stay at home with their children and create a perfect environment. They were to be ready at the door, beautifully turned out with ribbons in their hair and wearing a clean dress, radiating tranquillity at the breadwinner as he came home at the end of the day. They were to fetch his slippers and newspaper before making him comfortable in front of the fire. I'm not sure many women see it that way now. Times have well and truly changed! When my husband Mike walks through the door he's greeted with the turmoil of family life in all its glory: children waving bits of paper and imparting snippets of news; an over-enthusiastic dog; and a wife who's in the kitchen invariably waving a spatula in a vain attempt to bring order out of chaos with half a packet of fish fingers.

> **Top Tip:** Distribute the household chores among whoever is old enough to wield a duster so that it's not all down to you.

If you have a partner and you both walk through the front door at the end of the day, come to some arrangement about the housework. The sad fact is that although both men and women go out to work, in many homes it's the woman who does the lion's share of the cooking and cleaning. Divide the chores up so you have an equal bash at things. If you have a partner who enjoys cooking, make him happy, let him do it! Encourage older children to get involved in the kitchen – it may be messy at first but will improve with time! Don't make too many hard and fast rules though. Be flexible – you don't want to end up arguing over whose turn it is to take the rubbish out while the dustbin quietly overflows into the house. Make a rota of what has to be done and get older children involved where you can. They can do jobs like watering the plants – kids will let you know when they need a drink . . . plants won't. There is no reason in the world why a mum should work as well as taking on the whole burden of domesticity.

Look for short cuts. If you're on the Internet at home, try doing the weekly shop from the comfort of your own surroundings by clicking buttons and sending your order down the telephone line. More and more supermarkets are offering on-line shopping so make the most of it, especially when you consider that, on average, you will spend a year and a half of your life wheeling a trolley round supermarket aisles. You may not be able to keep on top of household jobs as well as your non-working friends do, so prioritise what has to be done and don't feel guilty about what you leave for another day. If you can afford to farm out some jobs such as ironing, do it. Don't end up like the woman who was buried in Bushey graveyard with the epitaph:

here lies a poor woman who was always tired
for she lived in a place where help wasn't hired . . .

Work out what you're prepared to let slip in order to spend more time doing what's really important – spending time with your family. And if you're exhausted – go to bed. Know your limitations: you will have days when you feel like you do nothing but work and sleep, but that may be the only way to get through some patches. And trust me, it will get easier, physically, as your child gets older.

 Top Tip: *Do your best to focus your attention on your family and not the dust lurking under the bed.*

Pressure Cooking

Hot spots for mums tend to be first thing in the morning and that mad hour or two at the end of the day, so look for ways to get organised and take the lid off when the pressure builds. You could try a few of these tips:

- Have a designated place for important bits of paper that your child needs to take with her, such as homework and permission slips, and get her into the habit of always putting them there; you may also have to get yourself in the habit. My favourite trick is to throw an important letter away while claiming I've never received it.

- Try to get your child ready in plenty of time before you

79

leave the house; don't cut it to the last minute or you'll always be late and chasing your tail.

- The flip side of the coin is not to get your child organised too early or you'll find she's disorganised herself again by the time you leave. Believe me, you will have no chance of success twice in one morning!
- Aim to spend as much time as possible with your child when you get in from work. The most important thing you can do is to give her time; not 'quality' time, but simply time. Aim for time that is not squeezed to the last drop with a sense of urgency or achievement: time that is not pressurised with an air of 'now or never' about it. And remember that children don't have to sit still in order to hold a conversation!

Don't bombard your child with questions and don't expect too much from her when you get home. The information she chooses to tell you may not be what you really want to hear; she may rush to tell you about one of her class mates getting into trouble when you'd rather find out how she got on with her spelling test. Your child may not spill the beans on the really important things that have happened until bed time. Recognise that she may not want to have a heart-to-heart with you as soon as you walk through the door, she may want to go out and see her friends. It's not a case of rejection, it's just what every child does! Be there for your child to talk to in her time, not yours. You'll be tired after a day at work and you'll also need some time to adjust. Build in routines that you can all look forward to as a way of unwinding together. Try to set aside an evening a week which you can spend together as a family and which doesn't involve running a taxi service to and from after-school activities.

80

Cook the kids' favourite meal or get a take-away, take the phone off the hook and do something you all enjoy.

Everyone's a Winner?

What you will miss most as a working mum is leisure time. Saturdays will undoubtedly be riddled with trips to the dry cleaners, the library or to the shops to buy all the odds and ends you can't pick up from the supermarket. You may end up feeling that you've spread yourself so thinly that you're not achieving anything at all. That's when it's even more important to take some time off. You will have to make an effort to create space and time for yourself. Don't neglect yourself or you'll end up feeling like an overworked machine. If you have a partner make sure that you share responsibility for your child and don't feel bad about doing what you want for a change, even if it's only time enough to wax your legs. I've ended up several times with one leg looking like the Black Forest and the other resembling a tropical rain forest *after* the lumberjacks have paid a visit. And if you're lucky enough to get offers of help from friends or relatives, don't turn them down.

 Top Tip: *Gratefully accept any offers which allow you to have some time to yourself.*

We went along to a craft fair recently where, among all the pots and jewellery and wooden ducks, we found a circus stall.

Everyone had great fun staggering about on stilts and juggling bean bags, but what we ended up bringing home with us were a couple of plates on sticks, carefully chosen by Benjamin and Joseph to match Arsenal's home and away colours. We had lessons on how to spin the plates, and jokingly we were told it would take a lifetime to achieve. The plates were made of plastic, which was just as well, as none of us could master the easy spinning bit, let alone the 'balance the stick in the cleft of your chin and spin it' bit. Falling plastic plates may not smash but they can still inflict bruises. Quite what the fascination was for plate-spinning I don't know. I suspect the children were hooked because, done by an expert, it looks so easy; the reality is quite different.

Unfortunately that's where the similarity ends with the juggling of work and family commitments. The joy of plate-spinning is that you can give it up any time you like, and the plates are plastic so you needn't have an emotional trauma every time one comes crashing to the ground. To juggle work and family you need to take a much longer view. Accept that you will mess things up and then have another go – without getting too despondent. There's a line from the film *Toy Story* that comes to mind. After Buzz's remarkable demonstration of his own flying ability, Woody says, 'That's not flying, that's falling with style.' Being a working mum may not mean that you can fly through life with the greatest of ease, but you can certainly fall with style.

'It's Life, Jim, but Not as We Know It'

How Do I Organise Weekends and School Holidays?

Madonna was recently quoted as saying that what she wants most is to be 'remembered as a good mother'. And I guess if we were interviewed by the world's press, most mums would come up with something similar. Being a mum is a seven-day-a-week job and that means, whoever you are, weekends and school holidays are a big test. Before you had kids, weekends used to be an oasis from the hustle and bustle of everyday life, but now . . . ! And that's one of the main problems – we all look forward to having a break at the end of the week but instead we exchange getting the kids to school and back for ferrying our offspring to parties, sleepovers and the bowling alley.

How many weekends end up with parents having rows and

children asking 'What are we going to do next?' It all starts first thing Saturday morning when you were hoping for a lie-in. If you are at home with the children all week you may be looking forward to your child's father taking over the responsibility for a few hours. He, on the other hand, may be hoping to unwind without the kids. Organise together what you're going to do, so you don't get the weekend off to a bad start. But don't plan to do too much; it's no rest if you're twice as busy. A bit of organisation can prevent a skip load of recriminations.

Make the weekend a family time, rather than seeing it as your time which is being invaded by children. Decide to have fun together rather than end up with a child who feels that the only way to have a good time is to keep out of Mum's way. Explain to your son or daughter that you want to enjoy Saturday and Sunday as much as they do and that everyone will appreciate it more if you are relaxed and have time to put your feet up with a cup of tea once in a while. Plan to have short periods to yourself so you can recharge your batteries, especially if you're raising children on your own. And if the plans don't work out, unashamedly grab some peace and quiet when your child is involved in doing something that doesn't require input from you.

 Top Tip: *Encourage children to make their own amusement some of the time – you don't have to become a children's entertainer all weekend long.*

There is no need for you to suddenly become a full-time all-singing all-dancing children's entertainer. You are not there

84

solely for the amusement of your children, however much they may insist that's the case. Relaxation time cuts both ways and should be available for mums as well as their offspring. Encourage your child to make his own entertainment for at least part of the day, even if it means you have to spend a few minutes or so getting him involved in something that doesn't require your total undivided attention. For younger children it can be something simple like laying out a roll of old wallpaper in the garden, patterned side down, giving them pots of paint and paint brushes and setting them off to create the biggest painting ever. If you have an only child it's a good idea to arrange for one of his friends to come round for a morning or afternoon even if they end up doing nothing much together.

How Many Weeks?

The two words 'school' and 'holidays' are enough to strike fear into the hearts of even the strongest, most saintly mothers. Visions of bored children and rainy days fill your head. Strangely though, taking an overview, from a distance with one eye shut and squinting into the sun, I like the school holidays. I enjoy taking life at a more relaxed pace and, as I work from home, I enjoy getting up later and feeling free to wander round the house in my dressing gown until I'm ready to face the day. I especially enjoy the long summer holidays when bedtime does not have to be strictly enforced and we can all take advantage of summer evenings. But there are still a few aspects of the school holidays I'm not so keen on.

I don't like the fact that over the last few days of term the children become demob happy so that when they break up they're hyper. This in turn leads to a settling down period right at the beginning of the school holidays which is pretty traumatic. The children don't know what to do with themselves once the structure of the day has changed and they generally wind each other up, while I can't face the prospect of six weeks of bad behaviour. Neither do I like having so little uninterrupted time to myself while my children complain that they're bored and persistently ask me what's for tea, lunch or whatever meal they feel they ought to be having. I usually end up crossly telling them that I would love to have enough time to be bored (which, even I realise, is about as useful as boiling an empty kettle). I also get fed up with the fact that I feel solely responsible for my children's amusement for several weeks. Dressing up each day as Coco the clown wears a bit thin after the first week or two.

Those Were the Days . . .

Children are quite often ratty at the beginning of the holidays. They've gone from having each day mapped out and being told exactly what they should be doing to what appears to be total liberty. And it goes to their heads! Overnight they're faced with freedom from structure and they don't know what to do with it. The dark winter holidays are often worse as you are all cooped up together indoors much more. It doesn't help if you fill the first few days of the holidays with loads of activities as you only delay the inevitable. Give children a bit of space even if they moan at you because they're bored. Give them time to wind down. Hang on to the fact that once they've settled down, you'll all be able to enjoy the freedom a bit more.

 Top Tip: Be prepared for a settling-down period at the beginning of the holidays when your child has to adjust to a different routine.

But what do you do with bored children for six weeks, or longer? If you've got a school-age child and you're out at work you've got the added problem of finding child-care facilities for an extra six hours a day. Your child-minder (if you've got one) may be happy to look after them for a few extra hours. If you work part-time, see if you can swap child-care arrangements with another part-timer. You'll end up with extra children when you're at home, but they may amuse each other. Arrange your leave and your partner's leave to coincide with breaks from school, where possible. You may not spend as much time together as a family as you would like if you take it in turns to look after the children, but you'll cut down on the trauma of finding child care. If you're on your own you could make a similar arrangement with another single mum so that together you cover a large proportion of the holiday. School holidays are the time to enlist the help of relatives (if you're lucky enough to have them) who would love to have the kids to stay for a week. Look out for locally run courses during the holidays. There are lots of two-day/whole-week courses in everything from football to orchestra practice. Many of these courses are very reasonably priced and you'll at least know that your child isn't bored while you're slaving away.

If you've got the whole stretch to do on your own a bit of planning works wonders. Try to arrange a few trips out every week so that the days are broken up. It's tempting to plug the kids into the TV or computer and let them amuse themselves. That's OK for a while; there's no harm in children sitting quietly watching a programme that interests them. Our children have all enjoyed watching activity programmes which give them something practical to do afterwards. There's a knock-on effect from this, however: I've never been *quite* so enthusiastic about the prospect of having to suddenly rustle up three cardboard boxes, an empty washing-up bottle and fifteen elastic bands so they can start to make a windmill and leave me to finish it. But plugging the kids into the TV for hours at a time is not very rewarding for them or you in the long term (although, to be honest, I did find myself in the rather unusual position of having to ban chess once in favour of the telly because, being an *Alice in Wonderland* chess set, too many fights were breaking out over the loss of Tweedledee).

> **Top Tip:** Plan ahead in the holidays and keep a balance between organised activity and relaxation.

Ready or not, I'm Coming!

Look for different relationship-building activities to do together (this applies to weekends as much as it does to holiday time). One day in the middle of the summer holiday I had a wonderful idea to make paper mâché masks with my children. The blowing-up-the-balloon bit and tearing-up-the-newspaper bit was great fun for the children, but when we got to the stick-the-paper-on-the-balloon stage the children decided I was happily preoccupied and I was abandoned on the kitchen floor while they ran off and played hide-and-seek.

Find creative things to do that are inexpensive. Six weeks of summer holidays can be enough to send you bankrupt with demands for cinema visits, trips to the local farm or zoo and shopping expeditions. And taking the kids to do the weekly shop can be horrendously expensive as they lob into your trolley all sorts of goodies they've seen advertised on the TV – you can end up buying a new brand of cat food for the cat you haven't got. To make school holidays a bit easier/less expensive you could have a go at some of the following:

- Local libraries often have story times or book trails and may be able to help you with a guide of what's on in your area.
- You don't have to go out to the cinema – have the cinema at home. Buy some popcorn, hire a video and pull the curtains. You can even make tickets to 'sell' to your children and their friends. I've spent several happy afternoons dozing on the sofa while the children sat in the dark and watched the 1.30 p.m. and the 3.30 p.m. performance of a cartoon we hired.
- If your son or daughter wants to do something exotic like going out for a meal and it's just too expensive, have a special meal at home. Make them dress up as if they were going to the best restaurant in town, lay the table with the best crockery and light some candles. We've made our children go outside and ring the front door bell before showing them to their seats! Not only is it fun, but it's good practice as to how to behave when they're out for real.
- Draw up your family tree together. Children love to find out about how they're related to people, even if it gets a bit complicated. It's good for children to see where they fit into the extended family and they love asking questions about their background. Take the chance to talk to your children about your upbringing; they may ask you flattering questions such as 'Did you used to have candles instead of electricity?' or 'What was it like living with dinosaurs?'.

 Top Tip: *Try to create memories for your child which will long outlast the school holidays.*

Drawing up a family tree can lead into all sorts of interesting diversions. It was during one such afternoon session in the school holidays that I started talking to our children about my grandmother, their great grandmother. When she died my parents bought a magnolia tree and planted it in our back garden in memory of her. Several years later they were going to move house and a friend of my mother's offered to re-home the magnolia tree in her garden for them, rather than leave it behind. My parents agreed to this and the tree was carefully transplanted to a new front garden. Years later still, my mother's friend moved house and this time the magnolia tree was left. Telling this story to the children led us to look for the tree. We knew roughly where my mother's friend had lived and it wasn't far from where we lived. It didn't take very long at all to track down the tree and while the current owners know nothing of its history it has significance now to another generation as well as adding a different dimension to one afternoon in the school holidays.

- Keep your eyes open for free exhibitions, preferably ones that will interest children. I made the mistake of taking mine to a free art exhibition which we whizzed round in about five minutes flat and left the moment one of them announced in a horribly loud voice, 'This isn't art, it's rubbish!' So much for culture.
- Make a list of things that are easy to collect then set your child off on a treasure hunt whereby he has to bring you one of every item on a list. The list can consist of all sorts of things and, if you're clever, the treasure hunt can be spread out over the whole of the holidays. Give your child a shoe

box to put his treasure in. For younger children make it simple with treasure such as a postage stamp, a leaf, a flower, a grey pebble etc. For older ones be a bit more inventive and plan what they collect around where you live but don't make it so difficult that they can't find anything.

- Visit local places of interest. Find out from your nearest library what's around in your area. You may well be surprised.

- Encourage your child to start a new hobby during the holidays. Talk about what interests him and go to the local library to see what you can discover. Children love collecting things – that's why football stickers and pop star photos are so popular.

- Arrange to go on a picnic with some friends. If the weather's bad have the picnic anyway. Spread a rug on the floor indoors and picnic there instead. With our glorious British summers you have to expect it to rain.

- If you travel everywhere by car, go out for a ride on a bus or a train. Reduced fares on trains mean it needn't get too expensive and you don't have to go very far – a few local stops is often far enough; it doesn't need to be a whole-day excursion.

- Go to the park, go for long walks, visit farms for children – but not all on the same day! Save some excursions and some of your energy for different times during the holiday.

- Join in that game of hide-and-seek with your children!

We've had many summer evenings that have ended up as family water fights. And they've all been fun until, of course, we've reached the point where someone goes one step too far and throws a bucketful of water out of the bathroom window onto Mum or Dad and it all ends in tears (normally Mum's or Dad's!). But that's to be expected. One very breezy holiday we spent a happy afternoon with friends balanced on top of a shingle bank. We all lined up on top of the bank, much to the astonishment of passers-by, held hands and did impressions of Rose in *Titanic* as she stood on the prow of the ship with her arms stretched out. The wind was so strong that we could lean right into it with our coats billowing out behind us. Fortunately, the sound of our singing was carried out to sea and only inconvenienced the gulls. We had to be careful in case the wind dropped suddenly, but it was great fun and cost nothing!

Bear in mind, however, that out of all that you do with your child during weekends or holidays what he remembers will probably be comparatively minor incidents. One Easter holiday was jam-packed full of trips and treats. When Mike and I went into school for a parents' evening a couple of weeks later, however, we were greeted by the unexpected in the children's ubiquitous News Books. One had drawn a glorious technicolor picture of me bending down having an iron injection. The caption explained that during the holidays we went to the doctors so mummy, who was pregnant, could have her injections. Another news story revolved around how we bought a goldfish and then took it to McDonald's for tea. All the effort I put into cinema trips, library trips and visits to friends – I might just as well not have bothered!

I Told You So

Mums with older children can become embroiled in the 'doing of homework' ritual during any one of the school holidays and more especially at weekends. This particular ritual reaches a climax just minutes before the child returns to school. It begins with the mum pointing out to the child that he has a project, some revision and a book to read and that it would be a good idea to plan out the aforementioned work so that it is finished in good time for Monday morning. The child may or may not agree that this is a good idea, but in any case, he will totally ignore this sound advice. Without fail, he will leave everything, in spite of repeated naggings, to 'the last minute'. Then there will be much wailing and gnashing of teeth and 'I-told-you-so's' and, before you know it, all the refreshment of a rest from routine has gone completely out the window. Along with, in some cases, the homework books themselves.

In an ideal world this ugly scenario would be avoided, but ideals are very seldom lived up to. Try and get your son or daughter into good habits. Encourage them without nagging and tell them 'well done' when they've made progress. Make space during the day so they're not rushed off their feet and don't have time to do anything. Try to help them organise their work without doing it for them, but if all fails try not to say 'I told you so' the night before it's due back. Above all try to be encouraging.

Top Tip: *Encourage children to be organised with their homework so you can all relax about it.*

'We're All Going on a Summer Holiday'

A family holiday in July or August breaks up the long summer holidays but can bring its own pressures. We're all aware of the financial strain that holidays bring but that's sometimes only part of the story. I recently read about a stress scale which measures and compares all of life's events. Going on holiday is only a couple of notches above 'minor violations of the law'! As mums bear the brunt of getting organised and packed it's a good idea to think ahead and avoid cramming clothes into suitcases at the last minute. Do all that you can to minimise the last minute mad laundry session so that you don't arrive on holiday comatose with exhaustion. One year the children went down with a stomach bug two days before our holiday. The day we left I caught it too, and while Mike packed the car, I had to cope with washing bedding, packing wellies and dashing in and out of the toilet being sick.

Finding a holiday that will please every member of the family gets increasingly harder as children get older and have their own ideas about what they want or where they want to go. Compromise is the only solution and that means that children have to compromise as well as adults. Look for places where there is a wide range of things to do but make sure that you have a rest as well and don't end up swapping one set of pressures for another. The week before we go away on holiday is always a fraught one. Our children become more and more excited while I become more and more tense as I battle to get everything ready. There are always pets to be sorted out, shopping to be done, a last-minute panic because the boys don't have enough socks (usually because the dog's eaten them – he's taken a particular fancy to boys' smelly socks), and that's without doing any packing.

 Top Tip: *Getting the whole family to help with holiday preparations will spread the burden and help them to appreciate what's involved.*

By the time it gets to the night before, I've had enough and I'm grumpy and bad-tempered. Mike comes home from work, looking forward to spending more time with his family, and is greeted by screaming children and a wife who's given up and is by now sitting in the middle of what looks like a jumble sale, eating a banana. It's downhill from there on in until we reach our destination. We always have the Packing Row – the 'why-is-there-so-much-stuff – we're-only-going-for-one-week' and the 'if-you-can-do-better-then-you-can-pack-next-time' sessions. Finally we have the Roof Box Row. This occurs when we're trying to manoeuvre a heavy roof box while still bickering over the jumble sale upstairs. Our friend Anne often house sits for us when we're away and her first question on arrival is whether or not she's missed all the arguments. Invariably by the time I've packed the children's stuff I find there's no room for my clothes and I end up wearing jeans and a jumper all week, even for the one meal out when everyone but me is togged up in their best clothes. Every holiday I vow it'll be less fraught but at the moment it's still 'Work in Progress'.

If you have a roof box to pack for holiday and you're not going abroad a good tip is to forget the suitcases and use black bin liners instead. Give everyone a bag and get them to pack their clothes in it. If it's done carefully the clothes don't get as squashed as in ordinary cases and the bags are far easier to pack in a square box. When you arrive it's very simple to give everyone their respective bin liner to unpack. You have to overcome the fear of looking like dustmen rather than holiday-makers, but it's worth it!

When you get to your holiday destination, listen to what everyone wants to do then pool ideas, dividing the day up so that everyone has a chance of doing something they want. Family holidays are often self-catering so make sure your child continues to help with domestic chores so that you can all have a break. Remind him that it's meant to be a break from routine for everyone and being on holiday is not an excuse to abandon all standards of hygiene and cleanliness. Whenever we go on holiday we insist that the children all do their fair share of unpacking. It doesn't take long. It also means that Mum isn't left to trail behind the rest of the family because she's been too busy stuffing T-shirts into drawers and cereal packets into cupboards little bigger than bird boxes to notice they've all gone swimming. The aim of your holiday should be that you *all* come back feeling refreshed and if everyone pulls their weight there's no reason why that shouldn't happen.

Weekends fly past too quickly – and there is a finite number of school holidays – surprisingly few when you look at the whole picture. Your whole life will not be littered with them, so make the most of them. Take a long-term view and aim to use the time as a way of building positive memories. Try to see it as an opportunity to be creative!

Top Tip: *Compromise is the key to all members of the family enjoying a holiday.*

'Christmas Is Coming and Mum Is Getting Tense'

If your family is anything like mine Christmas holidays pose a whole series of problems of their own. Not only have you got to keep your child occupied but you've got to do it while preparing for 25 December. As a mum you're undoubtedly busy enough without the run-up to Christmas. The build-up to a day – which is supposed to be a season of goodwill – can instead leave you with murderous feelings. The extra work that Christmas generates falls mainly on the shoulders of Mum who becomes the focal point for family, shopping and cooking the roast turkey.

Early preparation makes a big difference but the best-laid plans can fall apart! One autumn, when I was pregnant and prone to strange obsessive 'nesting', I was so far advanced with my Christmas preparation that I had bought and wrapped all the Christmas presents by the end of October. The presents were stashed safely in our bedroom and I was happy in the knowledge that come what may I would be ready by 25 December. One Tuesday morning a friend, Gill, and her daughter came round. Eleanor and Laura were three years old and good friends, having gurgled, crawled and toddled their way through life together. Gill and I had a coffee and chatted while the two girls pottered about as usual. We suddenly became aware that they had been out of sight and quieter than your average mice for a good half an hour. Time to investigate.

Eleanor and Laura were nowhere to be found downstairs so we went upstairs, by now a little concerned. My bedroom door was shut. We opened it and were greeted with the sight of two little girls delightedly sitting on my bed among a pile of wrapping paper and opened presents – Christmas had clearly come early. To make sure no one would see them they had shut the door, pulled the curtains and opened the goodies by the light of a bedside lamp. Gill and I both reacted in the same way. We looked at each other and walked out unable to keep straight faces. A quick conference was needed to decide what we should do before we went back in and told them both off. Laura was banned from sweets and Eleanor was not allowed to watch *Winnie-the-Pooh* for the rest of the week. Half an hour of hasty wrapping sorted most of the mess out but I was unable to stop Eleanor from telling everyone what they were going to get for Christmas.

Top Tip: If you can bear it, early Christmas planning will make life (a little!) less hectic in December.

You don't have to do your Christmas shopping in August to be organised but it certainly helps if you can think a few weeks ahead instead. Everyone gets stressed when they have to scurry round the shops on Christmas Eve like a demented ferret. So:

- Be practical and order things to be delivered if you possibly can. There are so many different catalogues around now and by making a few phone calls you may find you save yourself trekking around the shops for hours, with an over-excited child in tow. There are many charities who have catalogues full of Christmas cards and wrapping paper and ordering from them saves you leg work, as well as helping a charity. Catalogues often allow you to spread payments over a number of months although it's important to keep an eye on what you're spending and not allow your debts to get out of hand.

- Enlist some help from the rest of the family. If everyone does a bit to help then it's not so hard for you. Get them to help with the shopping rather than the 'Mum, can you get . . .' requests. There's no reason why you should have to shop, wrap, cook and write all the cards and end up feeling like the donkey which carried Mary to Bethlehem.

- Organise some space for yourself to enjoy the festivities in the run-up to Christmas.

- Cut corners where you can. If you're not a great cook don't ladle guilt over your head – look for food that's already prepared.

- Think about clubbing together with others to buy one (perhaps more expensive) present for an extended family member. Arrange with your in-laws (or outlaws!) who will buy a single present for whom on everybody's behalf. By creating a circle of presents each person receives one decent gift rather than twelve pairs of socks or bottles of bubble bath. And hey presto! Less shopping.

- If everyone's happy, don't be afraid to stop buying presents for some adults and only buy for the children. There's nothing worse than year after year buying and receiving half-hearted gifts.

- Don't take on any more than absolutely necessary in December – there's enough to do.

- Don't book up every spare moment with school concerts or shopping trips – you only end up frazzled. Arrange patches of time when you can unwind.

- Stop and take stock. Ask yourself why you're doing what you're doing. What is it that's important about Christmas to you? Is it all the glitter and tinsel or is it the chance to spend time with your family? It's easy to lose sight of the baby in a manger when you're stressed out.
- Make lists. Lists of lists if you have to; anything which gives you a clearer idea of what you need to achieve. Lists give you a focus and stop you feeling swamped with hundreds of non-specifics. And it's very gratifying to be able to cross off three items when you've done them; in fact I always include a couple of things I've already done just to give me a head start!

 Top Tip: *Making lists will give you some sense of control over what you have to do but don't lose the list once you've written it!*

Please, Please Me

Adverts encourage us to expect more, but it's often the inflated ideals which we, and our children, can never live up to that cause us the most problems. Not only will we not completely please our children but they most certainly will not please us! Ours was the only child in the pre-school nativity who refused to wear an angel outfit and sat, dressed in salmon pink, among the glittering tinsel of wings and halos with the grumpiest expression you have ever seen. I sat in the audience willing her to at least smile, not knowing whether to laugh or cry.

Be realistic at Christmas. Mums and dads spend thousands of pounds buying the latest and the best when five-year-old Sophie is happy just to play with the cardboard box the present arrived in. Presents are great and I'm the first to demand mine at seven o'clock on Christmas morning, if I can wait that long. At the end of the day, though, the toys are all forgotten and what's remembered is a time spent together with family and friends. There are very few presents that survive a lifetime of memories. Some of the plastic toys won't even see the holiday season out. So concentrate your efforts on making the memories count.

 Top Tip: *At Christmas concentrate your efforts on making the memories count.*

We have so many glowing fire/tinsel/mulled wine/mistletoe notions of what a good Christmas should be like, but the reality is often different. Your child wakes up in the middle of the night and wants to open his presents before you've even gone to sleep. You can spend hours making two dozen mince pies with a Santa's Little Helper in tow, knowing full well that you could knock the whole lot off in twenty minutes on your own. Don't be tempted to forfeit time with your child in favour of efficiency. If you do, although you'll want him to remember nostalgic Christmases, what will actually be imprinted on his mind is the fact that Mum thought he was a nuisance because she was busy.

I spent hours sitting with our six-year-old helping him painstakingly to write twenty Christmas cards to his friends at school. I could have done the job in five minutes on my own but I wanted to encourage him to do it himself. All the time I was trying not to think about how I hadn't bought any food or crackers yet and how the longer I left it the more crowded the shops would be. The cards were written and we were both pleased with the result. The next day I wasn't so pleased when we couldn't find them. Not anywhere. That evening we went through the whole process again (we found the cards, six months later, posted down the back of the radiator). Although less than amused at the time, with hindsight I'm glad I did it. The time invested in helping my son to do something that was important to him was far more valuable than all the trimmings I hadn't bought.

 Top Tip: *Ask yourself why Christmas is important then keep your answer at the centre of your preparations.*

Accept that Christmas will be less than perfect. Unless you have a very quiet Christmas on your own there is bound to be more than the usual amount of tensions and squabbles. So often, at Christmas, Mum is worn out trying to cook a dinner for fifteen while mediating between Auntie Anne who is eighty-six and can't cope with too much noise and nine-year-old twins who are running round the house shooting each other with laser guns. And all the time she's expected to stay smiling, look gorgeous and deliver the perfect meal – beautifully cooked and bang on time.

Don't shoulder the responsibility for things that are not your fault. Mums often take it upon themselves to be the creators of family harmony. When the harmony ends up more akin to the chants of rival football teams, however, we feel guilty. It's not our responsibility to keep everyone cheerful. Oil the wheels of diplomacy but remember the wise words that you will not please all of the people all of the time.

Spend Christmas with someone different. Last Christmas we had our Australian friend Colin to stay. A week before Christmas Colin asked us if he could bring along one of his flatmates who was on his own, a New Zealander called Ian. We also had a friend's Netherland Dwarf rabbit called Smokey to stay. It was not the usual combination of house guests but it was refreshingly different and all the children really enjoyed having such a cosmopolitan Christmas. Remember it's people not presents that make Christmas.

 Top Tip: *Christmas can be stressful for everyone so go easy on yourself and be prepared to do things a little differently sometimes.*

'Which Part of "No" Don't You Understand?'

How Do I Say 'No'?

Unlike 'capitulation' from which you can make numerous words (my friend tells me there are 288) there's a clear limit to the number of words you can make out of the letters 'n' and 'o'. But when you're standing in a toy shop calmly telling your child 'No', she can't have the latest 'must-have' toy on the market – a real snip at £50 – you may begin to wonder if:

a. Your child has heard you but has chosen to ignore you.
b. The word 'no' actually means something completely different to the under 16s (and the over 16s in some cases).
c. Your child has gone deaf.
d. You have accidentally started speaking a foreign language and you are the only one who understands it.
e. Your child has been abducted by aliens and replaced by an

exact replica but which is really an incompletely programmed hologram.

Saying 'No' can become a nightmare. How many times do you have to say that word in order to communicate a simple fact to your child? Until you have a child to look after, you never fully grasp what reaction that little word can create. Neither can you grasp the depth of feeling that it can unleash. And why can such a simple word be so difficult to understand? If your child is still a baby get some practice now: walk round any shop, look at all the wonderful packaging and say 'No' to yourself – very firmly. Alternatively, patrol the biscuit tin thirty minutes before a meal chanting 'No you can't have a biscuit, you won't be able to eat your dinner'. You'll be surprised how, before long, you'll sound like an old hand.

There are so many phrases that you swear you'll never use when you become a mum; phrases that have rung in your ears throughout your childhood. But once you've got a mobile child it all comes flooding back and there you are sounding like an old recording of your own mother. I was running a poetry workshop for a class of seven-year-olds recently and we were writing a poem about the weather which included repetition of the words 'I want'. When I asked the class what they wanted to do with the rain one boy answered that his mum always said 'I wants don't get'. That one familiar phrase could have easily derailed the whole workshop.

 Top Tip: *Choose the battles to fight with your child – some issues are not worth all the hassle.*

Order, I Say Order!

Giving children a positive upbringing does not mean you have to agree to all their demands. Don't fall for the lie that indulgence is the only way to prove you love your children. Children need to learn how to make choices for themselves and in order to do that they'll have to discover, pretty early on, that they can't have it all and they can't have it now. They need to know that they're surrounded by loving boundaries. Children feel secure when they have structure and order in their lives – when they know what is acceptable, considerate behaviour and what isn't. Decide on boundaries for your child's behaviour and stick to them. Let her know that pulling the cat's tail is not on, even though it may sway invitingly near the highchair. But don't be surprised when your child crosses the line anyway – just to test your reaction and see if you really mean what you say. How many 'Keep Off the Grass' signs have been taken as an invitation? The answer is to think beforehand about what you'll do in these types of situation.

Think carefully about the battles you fight with your children. There are some that are just not worth the bother. There will always be larger problems that will loom on the horizon, so compromise where you can over issues that are really very minor in the whole scheme of life. Both of our daughters wanted their ears pierced way before the age I was allowed to have mine done. We had to decide whether to let this become The Big Issue whereby they would rush out as soon as they reached the designated age and have every conceivable part of their bodies pierced, or whether to find a way to compromise. In the end we agreed that they could have their ears pierced once when they were seven but that they would have to wait until thirty-four if they wanted them pierced again, thirty-four being the age at which I had my ears pierced for a second time (though I fear we're about to start renegotiations).

There will be times when you need to stand your ground: when you need to say 'No' and stick by what you say. Your child will have a greater respect for your decision to stand firm if you don't make a big deal out of every petty problem.

If you mean 'No' keep to it, however hard your child tries to convince you that you really mean 'Yes'. Don't give in to an angry child's unreasonable demands. And certainly don't give in after she's kicked and screamed for half an hour. All you'll be doing is sending out the message that if she makes enough fuss she'll get her own way – eventually. There is no doubt that sticking to your guns can be extremely hard work. However, don't be put off – once your child learns that you mean what you say you will both benefit. And if you intend to let your child have what she wants, it's better to do so right at the beginning and not half way through a seven-day war or a screaming fit.

 Top Tip: *Try to be consistent. If you say 'No', do your best to stick to it.*

The Right Consistency

Psychologists have shown that gamblers find it hard to break the habit because they never know if the next bet will be their

big break. The next 100 to 1 horse they back with borrowed money will be the winner. It's the unpredictability factor that causes all the problems. If a gambler knew for sure that, whatever horse he backed in the next race at Kempton, he was going to lose, he'd be far less likely to carry on. But with any sort of gambling there's always the chance, however small, that you hold in your hand the winning ticket. It's the same with children when you're not consistent. If you say 'No' six times and then on the seventh you say 'Oh all right then' you're giving them the message that if they continue whining and nagging they may get what they want. Learn to take the unpredictability out so that your child knows precisely where she stands.

You need to be prepared to plug away at the same problem indefinitely and remember not to change the rules of the game half way through. Imagine a football match where the referee changes some of the rules without telling the players: suddenly it's acceptable to pick up the ball and run with it and filthy fouls are no longer sending-off offences. It wouldn't take very long for the game to break down completely and a riot to break out – and the referee would undoubtedly be the target of more than a few well-chosen words from the players and the crowd! It's hard work sticking to boundaries but it pays off in the end. For example if it's no ball games in the house then stick to that. They may try to bend the rules – mine invite friends round and use a pair of screwed up socks with the explanation, 'But mum, it's not a *football*.' I have to be very specific about certain rules and classify a ball, for the sake of law and order, as any object of any shape that can be kicked or thrown. Be one step ahead of the game; children will find any loophole to unravel your rules. Remember that children do not grow into sensible, reasonable, upright citizens overnight.

He's Got a Bigger One than Me!

Peer pressure can seem overwhelming to a child; pack mentality rules among groups of youngsters. All your child's friends have got the latest gadget except them – or so she'll tell you. It's worse than keeping up with the Joneses. We live in a society where ownership = well-being. If you have the right brand of washing powder, microwave oven, the correct breakfast cereal or a mini CD player you feel good. If you have every latest postmodern gadget on the market you feel good. If you have 2 cars, 1.7 children and 1.5 cats you feel good. And children are as susceptible to the advertisements as adults.

Top Tip: Remember that presents and love are not inextricably linked. You can show children you love them without spending a week's wages on the latest fad.

And peer pressure doesn't just stop at ownership. Children are also very good at noticing differences between people. They have keen observational skills and spot things that pass us by completely: they play Spot the Difference for real and not just in a puzzle book. Children don't like to stand out from their friends – they may feel they're different if they don't get the same as their best friend for Christmas. That's when the pressure gets transferred onto Mum or Dad. You can end up feeling that in order to show your child you love her you have to give into her every demand. But if you start equating love with buying expensive presents you'll soon find you've stepped onto a downward spiral. Encourage children to appreciate their own uniqueness and to express their own individual personality. Explain that it's the differences that attract you to one person rather than another – point out that it would be a very boring world if everyone was the same.

When I was a baby my godfather gave me a Bible; inside he had written a letter to me to read when I was older. One of the paragraphs talks about my parents and says this: 'They cannot, neither should they, give you everything you *want* – but they always try to give you everything you *need*.' There is a big difference between wants and needs. Of course it's wonderful to be able to give your child her heart's desire, and most parents do their best to achieve that, but there's a difference between a one-off special birthday present and a never-ending string of crazes that will end up driving you crazy. And not every parent can afford the latest electronic talking hippopotamus or a 4×4 remote-controlled car. Birthday parties can become a similar bone of contention. Once children are old enough to appreciate that some of their friends have parties in a hall with a children's entertainer and bouncy castle the pressure starts. You need to decide what sort of birthday party to give your five-year-old and not get sucked into a never-ending circuit of keeping up with everyone else. Do what your pocket and your nerves can afford.

We went through a phase when we, apparently, were the only parents in the whole world who hadn't taken their children to Disneyland. And what rotten parents we were because of that. Rushing to take out a second mortgage to pay for the trip would have only solved the problem temporarily as, no doubt, every other parent in the world would move on to even more exciting holidays. We would have ended up being the only parents who failed to buy a timeshare on the moon . . .

 Top Tip: *Children respond well to honesty even if they're disappointed so don't be afraid to explain to your child why you've said 'No'.*

Tell your son or daughter that you love them but that you can't afford to buy a particular present or that you don't think it's a wise thing to buy. Children respond well to honesty even if they're disappointed. If you can afford what they want but don't think it's a good idea, again you should explain your reasoning. After all, you are there to guide your child wisely, not to give in to every whim and passing fancy. If going shopping becomes a battlefield over what she wants to buy and you can't afford, try to avoid taking your daughter with you rather than repeating the same escapade week in week out. If you have to take children food shopping tell them they can have only one treat (with a price limit) so they must choose carefully. Children can cope better with disappointment if they understand your thinking, even if they don't agree with it. It's far better that they have an explanation than believe that 'No' is just one of *your* passing whims.

Teach your child the value of money. Give her a few pence to buy herself sweets when she's little and she'll soon start to understand that money is not made of elastic. Our children were all delighted in receiving odd pennies until they were old enough to realise that you couldn't actually buy very much with just one. Encourage your child to save for something she really wants by putting aside pocket money and doing odd household jobs. We live in an instant world: coffee, fast food, scratch cards, when in reality some of the best things in life are the ones worth waiting for.

The Sun Ain't Gonna Shine Anymore

While it's a great idea to involve your child in whatever you're doing, there are also times when a small child's help is a hindrance and you just have to say 'No'. If you involve your child as much as you can in your daily life – let her help you wash the car or clean the windows – then it's easier for her to accept you don't want her help when you're paying the bills and adding up a long list of figures. It's a sad fact that you can't forever protect your child from disappointment, however much you may want to. So the best that you can do is enable your child to handle the ups and the downs.

Perhaps the hardest 'No' I ever had to say was when one of our children's best friends was leaving school. It was an abrupt decision following a period of great difficulty for the family involved. I knew that we were very unlikely to stay in touch, however much we wanted to. When our daughter came out of school with the news I knelt down in the playground and let her sob on my shoulder. But when she asked me if we were likely to stay in close contact I had to say 'No'. She already knew the answer to that question and I knew that I wouldn't be doing her any favours by making promises I was powerless to keep.

Top Tip: *Continually indulging your child will not prepare her for life's disappointments.*

There are times when you'll say 'No' and realise later that you should have said 'Yes'. It's easy to slip into the habit of always being negative rather than positive, especially when you've got several small children making demands and you haven't got the time or the energy to weigh each request on its own merit. My friend Claire picked up her son, Jonathan, from school after one of the school's fundraising days. Jonathan told her that they'd been rolling pennies to raise money for the school. She asked him if he'd enjoyed doing that and Jonathan replied that he hadn't been able to roll any pennies as when he'd asked her for some coins that morning she'd said 'No'. Claire had been so overloaded that she couldn't even remember him asking!

There are many times when I've answered questions that I don't remember hearing. Children become very adept at raiding the fridge or the cupboards when you're on the phone. When you're distracted a nod of the head can be taken to mean anything they choose. In reality you are never going to be aware of everything that's going on so a little flexibility is required.

Continual requests for sponsorship and fundraising at school can drive even the most supportive parent to despair. And while it's good to get behind your child's school you may just get fed up with letters home about cake stalls and bringing in bottles for the school fair. One busy mum went into her daughter's school at the beginning of the academic year and gave the headmaster a cheque for £100 with the explicit instruction that she did not want to see a single letter about baking cakes, sponsored walks or selling raffle tickets for a whole year. A nice idea if you've got a hundred pounds to spare! Constant demands from any source can push you one step nearer the edge, so help where you can but don't be afraid to say 'No' if you really can't. And that goes for family events as well as school events. If you haven't got room for sixteen relatives to come and stay and you can't face the prospect, say so. Don't suffer in silence and spend the whole of Christmas in the kitchen smelling of burning martyr.

It's mums who usually take the brunt of having to say 'No' over everyday issues. They're the ones who tend to pick up the pieces of disappointment as their child's bottom lip starts to quiver. If you have a partner share the responsibility for making decisions, and over more important questions make sure your child understands that it is a joint decision. You need to convey a united front in order to prevent the situation where your child goes to each parent separately in order to get the answer she wants. Agree that you won't undermine each other's authority – if one of you has said 'No', then stick to that even if you have a quiet discussion later. Children quickly learn if one parent is more likely to say 'Yes' and will consequently try to bypass the other.

Top Tip: *Children can become adept at playing one parent off against the other so do your best to convey a united front to your child.*

Saying 'Yes' is always more gratifying than saying 'No', so look for opportunities to do so. Give children choices rather than ultimatums so that they learn to take responsibility for their actions. And while routine is really important to a child, the well-chosen break from normality becomes out of the ordinary and exciting. We travelled back from Scotland late one night and at the beginning of the journey the younger children asked if they could stay awake until we got home which would be about midnight. We said they could stay up if they could manage it. They were pretty bleary-eyed by eleven o'clock and had to work really hard at staying awake, but they thought it was great staying up so late and still remember the journey. Strangely, they've never asked again. It's the time you agree to one of your child's requests which is likely to be remembered long into the future, so don't be afraid of being charmed by your child into saying 'Yes'. Enjoy an unexpected moment once in a while.

PART THREE: PROGRESS

What I Really, Really Want!

How Do I Avoid Being Taken for Granted?

It's wonderful when someone appreciates you: not because you've just painted their bedroom or mended their clothes, but because of who you are. It doesn't happen very often as finding fault is easier than giving out pats on the back. Mothers' Day is an exception and a welcome one at that. In 1999, thirteen million cards were sent by post to mums all over the country. And of course that doesn't take account of all the handmade – still sticky with glue – cards that children lovingly pressed into their mums' hands along with plates of toast and cups of tea.

Mothers' Day should be celebrated, in spirit if nothing else, far more often. The improvement in my children's attitude was marked, although slightly marred by a comment in one of my cards which stated that Chelsea (the football team I support, but which most of my family don't) had slipped down a place in the league 'so there'. Mums do so much for their children, out of a mixture of love and necessity. On the whole you don't expect to be thanked every five minutes, and after all – by default or design – *you've* chosen to have a child so it's *your* responsibility to be a taxi service or a knee plasterer. However, being taken for granted is another thing altogether. And feeling taken for granted can hurt more than standing barefoot on a toy aeroplane.

Mum is often seen as part of the furniture, a comfy chair that's always there, reliable and safe. The problem is that mums don't always want to feel like comfy chairs. Inside my head somewhere I'm still seventeen; there are times when I'd rather be up in a hot air balloon than sat upon. And there are those crazy moments when I'd like to be someone else altogether – Lara Croft for example.

 Top Tip: *Being a mum and being taken for granted don't have to go hand in hand! The moment you start to feel put upon it's time to say something.*

Early One Morning

A few years ago a shopping trip made me realise just how taken for granted I was feeling. I got up one Saturday and rather than ruin the whole morning with a week's shop, I set out at the crack of dawn to do the shopping on my own. I skipped breakfast, left the children playing happily upstairs and a husband who was just entering the land of the living. Everything went swimmingly well: the shelves were full, the shop empty and I even found a trolley with all four wheels pointing in the same direction. I returned home rather smugly and should have recognised impending doom when the dog failed to give me his customary welcome and slunk off into a quiet corner.

I struggled in with fifteen plastic bags, straining at the handles, apparently unnoticed. Spirits dampened, but not extinguished, I ventured into the lounge to greet my children. It looked as if there had been an all-night party going on. A large cake had been freely crumbled around the furniture (what were they doing eating cake for breakfast?). Baby food had been spooned everywhere, but apparently not into the baby who was crawling round screaming blue murder with the remains of a nappy attached to his knees. Worst of all, soggy cereal had been trampled all over the house, snapping, crackling and popping as it went.

The joy of my self-sacrificial trip was beginning to evaporate as I dutifully got out the brush, dustpan, cloth, carpet cleaner and dustbin liners. The rest of the family seemed oblivious to the fact that my powers of self-control were being stretched to the limit and started asking for doughnuts, tea, squash and the newspaper. This was really too much. I began to shout, to no avail, so in desperation I picked up the nearest object to hand, which happened to be an apple, and hurled it down the hall against the front door. I found the squishy thud so satisfying that I fast bowled the remaining six down the hallway and, for the only moment in my life, stood a good chance of being selected for England's cricket team.

My explosion came as an enormous shock to everyone. As far as they were concerned I'd gone to get the shopping and had come home and behaved like a lunatic. They had no idea a concoction was bubbling away under the surface and that coming home to a house full of chaos added the final ingredient.

Allowing feelings of being taken for granted to build up is the surest way to create an unexpected explosion. It's vital to do something positive about those feelings as soon as you're aware of them. You can find yourself sinking under a heap of newspaper, crisp packet and biscuit-wrapper coupons in a bid to do your bit for the education system. And being taken for granted is not just for mums of small children. Having piles of

CAN I TAKE IT YOU NO LONGER WISH TO DO MY LAUNDRY - MUM?

dirty washing dumped on you by grown-up sons or daughters is just as bad, as is the unexpected visitor at meal times who expects to be fed. It's OK as long as you're happy to do the washing and stretch a meal for two into a meal for three – let's be honest, most mums are happy to do that. But the moment you start feeling put upon it's time to say something.

> **Top Tip:** *Allowing feelings of resentment to fester is the surest way to make you feel worse.*

Don't let feelings fester or multiply. Resentment is rather like the three stick insects you buy for your daughter. You hardly notice them at first but then one day they multiply and you find them all over the house, in the sugar bowl, swinging from the lights and lurking in dark corners ready to pop out and wave at you. Then you've got a problem on your hands. And believe me, seventy-three stick insects are a hundred times harder to ignore than three. The moment you're aware resentment is brewing is the moment to start talking.

Pardon?

Talk to a friend who will listen and point you in the right direction. If you have a partner tell him how you're feeling. The average married couple has four minutes of conversation a day. Four minutes, that's all. Quite how much of any significance you can convey in that brief moment, I don't know. You

123

may have to make an effort to express your feelings to each other. If you don't tell him, he probably won't guess and it works the same in reverse as well. You need to spend time together with your other half in order to understand the pressures that each of you face. Don't start a row by pointing the finger; instead be calm. The earlier you start to talk about your feelings, the easier it'll be to find answers to your problem. Focus on exactly why you're feeling put upon and take action to solve the problem. Don't generalise, be specific. If you feel that you're doing more than your fair share of child care tell your partner and make arrangements so that you can go out once in a while. Mums are often the built-in baby-sitter. Dads may take for granted the fact that they are able to go out on their own without having to fix up someone to look after the children. It's assumed Mum is always there. If Mum wants to go out she's got to make child-minding arrangements.

Let your son or daughter see you communicating with your partner. It's a good example for them to see you sharing problems as well as joys and it will encourage your child to talk to you. The 'don't-do-as-I-do – do-as-I-tell-you' approach does not work. Children copy what they see and hear, and subconsciously they absorb a lot more than we care to believe. If your child sees you bottling up anger, that's the role model you're giving him. If you tell your child off for swearing whilst swearing like a trooper yourself, guess what will be going on out of earshot? Whether you like it or not older children are far more likely to end up doing what you *do*, rather than what you *tell* them to do. Try to create a positive example. If children grow up in a house where there's lots of positive communication, they'll find it easier to communicate with you and others.

> **Top Tip:** *Talk about how you're feeling – and make sure you talk to the people who need to know.*

Children know instinctively when something's up – they can sense it in the air just as well as adults. If you're miserable because you feel you're being used as a doormat, they'll know you're unhappy even if they don't know why. Tell your child directly how you're feeling. If you feel as if your home is being treated like a hotel, work out exactly what behaviour is making you feel like that. Don't say it in an accusatory manner or generalise, but instead calmly tell him what's wrong. He may not be taking you for granted – he may think you're the best thing since 'Books for Schools' coupons – but he may just have forgotten to show you how much he appreciates you. The better your child understands you, the more likely he is to work with you rather than against you.

'I'll Tell You What I Want'

Never assume your son or daughter knows what it is you want in their behaviour. Tell them quite clearly what you expect of them so at least they know it makes you cross when they walk through the front door and dump a pile of bags and coats on the floor. Tell them how you'd appreciate it if they'd behave appropriately when Granny comes to visit. Tell them what you'd like for your birthday. If you don't give children any ideas you shouldn't be surprised that instead of receiving flowers, perfume and a novel by your favourite author, you end up with the *A-Z of Childhood Illnesses*, a tube of Superglue and a tin-opener. You will just have to be gracious, knowing they've done the best they can, and then go out and buy the bunch of flowers yourself.

I received a very strange assortment of presents one year: a box of chocolates (which everyone promptly ate), a temporary tattoo kit complete with coloured ink, some bubble bath, a Tribble, and a U2 video. Other than the requested video, the rest was down to the children. For several days I sported a two-tailed red and black tiger on my shoulder – the extra tail being added because the transfer had slipped.

Point out to your family that you do all the things you do because you love them but that prior warning of impending visits from older children at meal times would be helpful, as would a hand in bringing the shopping from the car or tidying up the mess they've created. If you're feeling put upon because your child is in and out without bothering to tell you when he's going to be around, then speak to him about it. Common courtesy is not too much to expect from any son or daughter. Explain that this is your home as well. Encourage children to take responsibility for their own washing or ironing once they're young adults; you do not have to spend your whole life being treated as the laundry maid.

> **Top Tip:** *Telling children what you want is often far more effective than dropping hints and hoping they'll work it out on their own.*

At the end of the day when we tidy up all the books and toys I try to organise children to do specific tasks. The problem is always that each child invariably has to tidy up something that is not his. They say the same thing every night – 'I didn't make that mess.' I always point out that I certainly didn't empty the contents of a box of Lego all over the floor and then play tiddlywinks with it so it's not my responsibility either but as we're a family we all help each other along. Working as a team, helping each other out, is the key. My friend Gill has a nifty reward scheme for the 'end-of-day tidying up' trauma. When the mess is cleared and the house is straight, she sits the children down and opens a packet of coloured sweets such as Smarties or jelly babies. Each child is given a sweet – if they guess the correct colour before receiving it, they get another one, and so on until they guess wrong, then it's on to the next child. I joined in once, arriving after all the work was done but before all the sweets had gone – great fun, though I think I was swizzled out of some of the sweets!

When I Grow Up

Spend time talking to your child, not only about what he thinks and feels but also about yourself; children are always interested in what Mum was like as a little girl. Share with him some of the weird and wonderful events from your past: the places you've been to that he doesn't know about and some of the naughty things *you* did as a child. He will probably be amazed! Talk to him as well about what you hope to do in the future, what you dream of doing one day. He may not even know

127

what your favourite colour is or what your favourite food is. By talking to your child about yourself you'll help him to understand that you exist in space and time outside the role of 'Mum' and that you're a person in your own right. He will see you as more than a mum – he may even have some useful suggestions for you. The more you communicate, the greater understanding there will be between you and your child.

PERHAPS NEXT TIME WE'D BETTER WARN MUM BEFORE MAKING AN UNEXPECTED SHOW OF APPRECIATION...

Another way of communicating is role-play. It works wonders as a means of showing your child how you are feeling. You don't have to take it seriously to get the message across either. Even tiny children enjoy swapping roles with Mum. Pretend that you're the baby and they're the parent and then behave accordingly (but don't get too carried away and remember any toys you throw you'll have to clear up). My children have all loved the opportunity to tell me I can't have biscuits or another mug of squash because it's nearly tea time, or the chance to insist that I go to bed at six o'clock without complaining. That's the point at which the game has to stop because if I lie down too early in the evening I won't get up again until morning! It's amazing how ten minutes of 'I wants' coming from you gets them acting out real irritation!

Top Tip: *Encourage your child to see you as a person in your own right and not just as 'Mum'.*

'Want Any Cheap Fish, Love?'

Imagine the kids have been really badly behaved, doing the exact opposite of what you've told them to do. You've caught them in the act and they're lined up to receive a really good grumble. There you are just about to deliver the punch line when the doorbell rings. Bedlam breaks out immediately, the dog barks, the children rush out of the room and by the time you catch up with the open front door, the kids have gone leaving you to deal with a man from Grimsby who is trying to sell you cheap fish. Five minutes later, the impetus has gone and you've missed the moment. By now the children have disappeared without trace, except for the youngest who's sitting quietly doing his homework – a picture of innocence. You may end up wondering why you bother at all. Interruptions are a fact of life, but they don't do much for your morale. We're plagued with them in our house – unwanted phone calls in the middle of meal times telling me I've won a holiday for two (and all I have to do is buy a timeshare); double-glazing salesmen who have missed the fact that the windows are already double glazed; the 'have you got five minutes for a market research survey' call. And that's without the happy interruptions of friends ringing for us or the children – there is no end. The more children you have the more likely it is that you will live at least part of your life in sound bites – moments of peace sandwiched between noise and disruption. Trying to hold it all together and maintain some semblance of order can leave you feeling like Robin with no sign of Batman in sight.

One of the most demoralising moments as a mum is when you're undermined. Whether it's deliberate or unintentional or from a string of unwanted interruptions, it still makes you feel rotten. Too many and you start to feel like a pattern on the wallpaper. Try looking beyond the immediate frustrations of everyday life. Take an overview and keep it all in perspective. Consider whether there might be a funny side to what's going on – don't always face life with a frown. There are moments when I feel I'm standing back and looking at my life from an outsider's view and it looks ridiculous. If we could only see ourselves as others see us we might not take everything so seriously.

Children grow up quickly so don't put your life on hold. While they're still ankle-biting think positively about what you will do when your son or daughter has left home. Make plans for what lies beyond the realm of small children and keep those plans in sight when you're feeling weak and weary. Most children will encourage their mums to hang on to their own lives as long as Mum isn't out every night of the week and the kids never see her.

Make a habit of telling your children that you appreciate them. Be positive and build them up. The more positive you are with your children the more positive they'll be with you. If they see you bad-tempered and nagging all the time, it won't give them much incentive to be appreciative. Teach your child to value and respect every member of the family as a person in their own right.

My friend Pearl is a grandmother. Every year on Mothers' Day she sends a card to both of her daughters because they are mothers in their own right, mothers of her grandchildren. It's a way of showing them that she appreciates and values her daughters in their roles as mums. So take time to show your children that they're important people in your life, even when they've got children of their own.

 Top Tip: *Tell your family you appreciate them – they may return the compliment!*

All Stressed Up and Nowhere to Go

How Do I Make Time for Myself?

Motherhood is a great leveller. It doesn't matter whether you've got wads of cash bulging from your purse or not a bean to your name, the one thing you won't have is time off. Unfortunately, you can't suddenly decide that you've had enough and you fancy a weekend in the sun on your own; wherever you go, junior comes too – in thought if not in person. And there's no doubt that taking time off is what every mum needs even if it's only for the odd half-hour. There was a time, long ago, when I decided to treat myself to a face pack. I'm not very good at beauty treatments as I don't seem to have time enough for it to work properly. Anyhow, a particularly fruity concoction caught my eye when I was out shopping so I bought it hoping that a face mask would make me sit down, even if it didn't take years off me.

I told the three older children that I was going to take my cup of tea upstairs and have some peace and quiet for half an hour. All the children were happily preoccupied so I disappeared while the going was good. I applied the lime green goo and lay down waiting for the mask to harden. Within five minutes the children started trotting up to see me, one by one, with various questions and complaints. It is very difficult to speak clearly when you have a face mask on but I had little choice and despite the fact that I was cracking round the mouth I managed to answer several questions before violently hissing 'Go away'. There was much sniggering and giggling as each child hovered in the doorway for one final look. That was until the youngest came up to see me. Joseph was only three and the sight of his mum looking like a cartoon creature was more than he could take. His bottom lip quivered as I feebly comforted him by saying that I wasn't feeling very well so I was having a lie down. He ran off crying and went to find a familiar face in the form of big sister Eleanor. Needless to say I might just as well not have bothered with the face mask as I ended up washing it off long before the allotted time. During the day when the kids are at school, or in the evening when they're all tucked up in bed is a much better time to do this sort of thing than at four o'clock in the afternoon. And the same goes for colouring your hair; if you put a hair dye on your head with children around, make sure you set the kitchen timer . . .

 Top Tip: *Try and set aside time for yourself – if you don't book it in it's unlikely to happen.*

You Can Run but You Can't Hide

When the children were smaller I used to sneak off to the bathroom for Five Minutes' Peace, pretty much like Jill Murphy's book of the same name. It was a great joy for me to be shut away from the hubbub, even if it was only for a few minutes. If I was particularly sneaky I could get into the bathroom without anyone noticing and I was guaranteed at least five minutes before they all came looking for me. This was all ruined one day when the children worked out that if they went into the back bedroom they could open the airing cupboard door and shout at me through the air vent that connected the bedroom with the bathroom. It was no fun sitting in the toilet with four pairs of eyes squinting at me through the gaps in the vent, so I exchanged this hidey hole, in good weather, for a spot at the bottom of the garden.

Available time slots change as children grow up. Once your baby settles down and goes to sleep at a reasonable time you'll get some time to yourself in the evening. If you don't go out to work you'll end up with the hours between 9 a.m. and 3 p.m. when your child is at school (and you'll be surprised how quickly those hours skate by) but you'll have no evenings. It gets increasingly harder to create free time as your child gets older and stays up later. You have to actively look for ways to find your own time, so:

- Insist your child is in her room, if not asleep, at a reasonable time in the evening. This gives her the opportunity to get a good night's sleep, especially on week days, and gives you the chance to unwind.

- Get a baby-sitter once in a while for an evening out and don't plan what you're going to do until you leave the house. When you haven't got children to cater for it's much easier to be spontaneous: doing something on the spur of the moment is a refreshing experience when you haven't got to worry about changing bags and pushchairs.

- Share lifts to after-school and weekend activities with other parents. Find another parent who travels to the same place at the same time and arrange either to take or to bring back. Going out once in an evening is infinitely preferable to going out twice.

Swapping Granny for a Dishwasher

Statistics tell us that the biggest increase in mothers is the over-thirties; more women are waiting until they're older to have children, waiting until they've pursued their careers or found the right partner. This means that grandparents also tend to be older and may be less able to cope with the demands of young children. Coupled with this, we live in a society which is no longer centred on the extended family. At the turn of the twentieth century responsibility for looking after small children was shared by lots of people including older brothers and sisters. These days families break up or move away and there aren't the close networks to help and support a new mum. Being a mum is not even the same as it was thirty or forty years ago. Then, most mums were expected to keep the house and children clean and little else. Life centred on the home and most of a child's leisure time was spent there as well. Visions of my grandmother shelling peas and spending hours digging up the daisies in the lawn with a blunt knife seem positively idyllic compared to my lifestyle. I frequently feel like the white rabbit out of *Alice in Wonderland* scurrying round with a watch in my hand to the tune of 'I'm late, I'm late, for a very important date. No time to say hello, goodbye, I'm late, I'm late, I'm late.'

 Top Tip: *If you can, build a support network of family and friends around you – there'll be more opportunities for you to have a break.*

Most of us have washing machines and microwaves but not all of us have parents who will come round and take the baby off in the pram to give us a break when we're dead on our feet with tiredness. Electrical appliances make our lives easier but they can't do the baby-sitting, unless you count plonking the baby in a chair in front of the washing machine while the coloureds go round. I often hear older mums saying 'In my day we didn't have all these gadgets, we had to wash everything by hand/put it through a mangle/take it down to the river', etc. etc. But they didn't have to charge around like today's mums: working, travelling further to school, cramming more into the day than is often good for them. No doubt we'll think our daughters have got it easy when they have children!

Support nowadays can come from friends as much as from family – mums with children of a similar age who are in the same boat as you. Friends can be a life-saver. You can make new ones if you:

- Find a local 'Parent and Toddler' group and go along – they're often held in church halls so there's bound to be one fairly close to home. Watching your two-year-old playing with other children the same age gives you a break from the constant demands and also gives you a chance to make friends with mums in the same situation.
- Help each other out. Do a baby swap and take it in turns to look after each other's children for a couple of hours once a week. It means that you get an extra child for a morning but the benefits of having some time to yourself in return more than outweigh a double dose of toddler.
- When the baby's asleep don't rush round like a lunatic trying to spring-clean the house. Make the most of it and have a rest – it is allowed!

Having said all this there is no need to go to the other extreme and do nothing all the time, however appealing Quentin Crisp's words are in *The Naked Civil Servant*: 'There was no need to do any housework at all. After the first four years the dirt doesn't get any worse.' Remember that you're trying to create an environment in which your child will be happy to grow up!

'All for One and One for All'

I recently read an article in the newspaper which talked about the fastest way to clean a house. It's based on an American idea whereby you work methodically, quickly and can knock off a two-bedroom flat in less than an hour. The answer apparently lies in making sure you've got the right tools for the job and that you do everything thoroughly and systematically once and don't keep going back over what you've already done. I haven't read the book this article was based on but I do know that if I get the whole family involved in this odious task, there's a chance we can get the house straight in a fraction of the time it takes me on my own.

There's an episode from *The Magic Roundabout* called 'The Clean-Up' where Dougal the dog decides the garden needs a good clean-up and that everyone is going to help him. This is optimistic when there are such characters as Dylan the rabbit who is rather like a spaced-out hippy. Needless to say, the vacuum cleaner goes out of control and sucks up Brian the snail before taking to the skies with Dougal going along for the ride. Getting the kids involved in a clean-up operation can seem to be more trouble than it's worth, but perseverance pays off eventually.

Encourage everyone to pull their weight. Rewards work wonders: 'If you help do the housework this morning, then we will all be able to go out somewhere this afternoon.' Children can earn extra pocket money for doing specific tasks. I have a very thorough duster who's happy to earn some money for doing the job I hate the most. And although Tooth Fairies seem to have upped their salary in recent years, the fee for extra household chores has remained reasonable. When they're older you should expect your son or daughter to be in charge of their own room and resist the temptation to spend your life clearing up after them. Not only do you benefit from getting the rest of the family to help but also the children get a better idea of what's involved in running a house. It's not as easy as they think and one day they may end up thinking twice before they walk through the house in muddy football boots – well, you can dream!

 Top Tip: *Enlist everybody's help at tidying up time!*

She Still Hasn't Found what She's Looking for

I have one tidy and one untidy daughter and mostly I leave them to get on with their bedrooms. I am not completely heartless or ignorant of health and safety regulations, however, so every now and then I tackle the bomb-site of a bedroom with a large black bag. Such behaviour is as good for our relationship as it is for hygiene standards. I don't continually nag her and we both end up with very positive feelings when the room is tidy. She is delighted to find three pieces of missing homework, her favourite necklace and about five pounds in loose change, and I am delighted not to have to keep her bedroom door shut all the time.

Don't waste your time trying to achieve the impossible and do not expect perfection from your children. They may well be untidy. Drum into them general standards of behaviour, then enlist their help. Praise them when they *are* tidy. In the words of Samuel Rogers, a nineteenth-century poet, 'Pleasure that comes unlooked for is thrice welcome'. It's a wonderful surprise to find that a kitchen full of unwashed cups has been tackled by someone else. And if you show your appreciation they might do it again. Set yourself realistic targets:

- Plan what you're going to do to keep the house in order and don't be tempted to try and do tomorrow's washing-up today!
- If you have younger children see if you can arrange for someone else to take care of them for a morning to give you the chance to do something for yourself.
- Don't feel guilty if a friend takes your child off your hands for a couple of hours and you do nothing except sit down and read a magazine. My friend Joyce had seven children and on the occasions her mother looked after the youngest, Joyce would put her feet up and read (much to her mother's amazement!). It did her more good than running round with a mop and duster.

 Top Tip: *Aim for efficiency when it comes to household chores. Work out what you can reasonably manage in one go then leave the rest 'til next time.*

A Little Bit of Time Goes a Long Way

There's a school of thought which says that 'man is more than the sum of his parts' and there are times when that phrase expresses exactly what I feel. Many of the jobs that mums do are mundane and repetitive: picking up clothes from the floor, doing the ironing, organising who takes what to school on what day, making packed lunches. You may feel that you are more than the sum of all the roles you play: partner, mother, daughter, sister, friend, neighbour. You may feel that there's a different person somewhere inside who's trying to get out through all the layers. The only way to allow that person to come out is to give yourself time to do some of the things that you want to do. The problem is that this can go against the grain when you're a mum; many mums think that doing anything for themselves is selfish.

I first took up writing when our youngest child was eighteen months and our eldest was seven. It was also the time when we had a stream of foreign students coming and going. Life was chaotic and passed by in a blur, to the extent that I didn't know whether it was 'Guten Morgen' or 'Bonne Nuit'. On the surface, it's quite a ridiculous time to start something new but I was feeling completely overwhelmed with small children, and French and German teenagers. One evening, when the house was fairly quiet I said to Mike that I was feeling bewildered and I wanted to do something different. A month in Barbados might have been a good idea, but instead we went through a list of all the things I wanted to do (such as become an airline pilot or climb Mount Everest). After crossing out most of my ideas we ended up with a short list of one – writing. I wanted to write and, what's more, given the constraints of family life, I was able to write.

Top Tip: *Don't give up all your interests or hobbies. Give yourself space to continue growing as an individual.*

I felt so much better with the prospect of something ahead of me. It was something I could develop, improve and which would, hopefully, develop and improve me. I have to say that at that point I had no idea *what* I was going to write, but the details were irrelevant; what was important was that I had a vision for life outside of children and packed lunches. Being a driven sort of person, I set myself targets – realistic goals that I hoped to achieve so I could gauge whether my writing would eventually turn into a career or whether it would simply be a carrot on a stick to get me through a hard patch. Despite having so much to do I made the time – the odd fifteen minutes here, the odd half-hour there – to sit down quietly and put pen to paper.

We all make time for the things we really want to do. It's amazing how much can be squeezed into a day. The saying is true that if you want something done you should give the job to a busy person. Someone who is busy always seems able to pack more into their lives. Jobs and chores expand to fit the time available and while you shouldn't aim to drive yourself into the ground, you'll be surprised how much you can get done in an odd fifteen minutes. So, find something that interests you and do it – whether it's scuba diving, parachuting, gardening or egg-painting. Arrange spaces in the day when you can pursue your hobby. Give yourself space to develop as an individual and not just as a mum; and as you develop interests that are not solely centred on the children you will become a more interesting, fulfilled person. While motherhood is a very rewarding and fulfilling experience you cannot expect to get everything you need emotionally or mentally from your family. Friends and outside interests will improve your quality of life and the less frustrated you are the better mum you're likely to be.

 Top Tip: *Find something that interests you – then do it!*

Bye Bye Baby

My cousin Annette celebrated one of her birthdays while on holiday. It coincided with the time one of her children was going through the 'need a poo, done it' stage. Despite the constant use of trousers with elasticated ankles to contain the problem, she often found herself and her son caught in embarrassing situations. On Annette's birthday, her husband Gary offered to deal with all the 'need a poo, done it' situations in order to give her a break. This may sound quite insignificant, but it's those kind offers which give you a rest from your share of the routine that keep you going. It makes you feel that there is life outside of small, unexpected piles on the stairs.

Look for opportunities to have a longer rest from the routine; it's worth it even if it means you have to put in some extra work to get it organised. Recently I was very fortunate to be able to spend a week in the Middle East visiting a friend, on my own. But in order to do that I had to spend a week getting all the household jobs up to date. I stuck a list on the kitchen cupboard of all the things that Mike had to remember to do – send a spelling book into school on a Monday, take the boys to Beavers and Cubs on a Thursday, and so on. The list filled a side of A4 paper entirely and ended with the phrase 'Be nice to each other'. One of the children said, before I went, that I was the oil which made the machine run smoothly and that she feared it would all come crunching to a halt if I wasn't there. But no one is indispensable and Mike managed perfectly well without me. There were no major disasters – they all looked reasonably clean when I got back and they assured me they didn't just live on beans on toast and takeaways. Not everyone can manage a week away, but even a day makes all the difference.

 Top Tip: *A break from routine can be refreshing if you're unable to get away.*

Lost in Space

We all need space around us. How much space depends on who is trying to get close to you. Julie says she can tell the age of a mum's children by the marks on her clothes: there's the vomit-down-the-back stains from a tiny baby; the sticky marks on the legs from a toddler; and the mucky finger-prints on the arm from the constant tapping of an older child. Immediate family members are allowed into the close proximity zone, which means you'll let them get within eighteen inches of you without breaking out into a cold sweat. Children, young ones especially, take great comfort from their mums being no more than a few centimetres away, but it can be annoying having someone constantly hanging onto your skirt.

You can find practical ways to get some space at home. Have a designated area that is yours where you shouldn't be disturbed, except in dire emergencies. You could have a bedroom as your space, or a chair, or if you're really pushed for space you could sit half way up the stairs. One eighteenth-century mother called Susanna, who had twelve surviving children, found a way of having a quiet time despite all the demands of a big family. She spent much of her time in the kitchen and when she needed space she would throw her apron over her head. This was a signal to her children to leave her alone and stop pestering her for a little while. Apparently it worked. So however tough it is there is always a way out!

Top Tip: *Try and create your own bit of space, however small, so that there is somewhere you can go to get away from it all.*

When a child interrupts you in the middle of some domestic chore, it pays dividends if you stop and pay attention to her. A couple of minutes spent listening intently and responding properly to your child will not only reinforce the fact that you love her and value her but it will also break the cycle of constant pestering and you will discover a few more minutes to yourself.

146

Going on holiday can be a good time to untangle yourself from the knot of children and can give you the chance to be more than two centimetres away from eager little hands. We spent one holiday in the New Forest. It was an eventful time, not because of sudden hospital trips or flat tyres, but because of the lack of space surrounding the holiday. We booked a 'chalet' in a hundred acres of park land which turned out to be little more than a shed – one of a thousand – and not much bigger than our one at home. There were six of us crammed into three tiny bedrooms with no room for cat swinging or, in fact, movement of any kind. The girls were wedged at night into bunk beds and you could only get into the bathroom sideways. I look forward to holidays and the chance to have more space than usual and so it was just awful. The children were all too young to be allowed outside on their own and we didn't even have the freedom of a garden. We constantly tripped over each other and there was nowhere to escape to for a moment on your own. We all needed the space, not just me, and by the end of the first day we were all edgy and irritable. I couldn't reconcile the fact that we had paid money for this and we were crammed together like unhappy sardines. In the end we could take no more and came home early. At least at home we had room to breathe and the gadgets which make life with four children a little easier.

Encourage your son or daughter to respect your need for some time to yourself in the same way that you give them space and privacy. So teach by example – if you remember to knock on a teenager's bedroom door she might think twice about barging into your room uninvited every five minutes. Remember that being a mum does not mean that your whole life has to be taken over – there should be some time in it for you as a person and not just as an extension of your children.

'Ring Me when You Get There'

How Do I Let My Child Grow Up?

I CAN'T BELIEVE MUM LET US COME BY OURSELVES WITHOUT MAKING A FUSS!

SCOUT CAMP

We've had several wasps' nests buzzing in or around the house over the years, but the worst, if not the biggest, was the one underneath the dining-room floor. At the time I didn't know that there was a time bomb sitting under the floorboards, but

I did notice some activity by the patio doors. I watched for a while and saw one or two wasps squeezing in through a tiny crack between the frame and the bricks before disappearing. They were clearly not coming into the house and as there are steps immediately under the doors I foolishly assumed the wasps were trying to find a home behind the steps.

A little knowledge is a dangerous thing but no knowledge at all can be fatal. Without consulting anyone I figured that the best course of action would be to repair the crack and stop the wasps from going behind the steps. And so began the battle. First of all I got some filler, but the wasps squelched through before it had set. Then I tried quick-setting filler but they painstakingly nibbled a hole into it as soon as it hardened (very interesting to watch). Mastic next – just as ineffective. Then I tried lateral thinking and put a hose in the crack and turned it on full blast. I nearly drowned and the wasps continued to buzz about, except that now, instead of one or two, there were about a dozen of them. Undaunted and totally fascinated with these creatures and their single-mindedness I tried filling the hole with sand. The wasps, in response, lined up, dug a burrow and in they went. The next morning it was chilly when I came downstairs. Mike had gone to work leaving the kitchen light on and I found the kitchen window blanketed, on the outside, with wasps. A startling sight, to say the least. Time to admit defeat and call the Wasp Man.

The Wasp Man arrived, took one look at my deterrent efforts and asked to look at the dining-room floor. The wasps' nest was not, as I had assumed, behind the steps, but under the floorboards and the wasps were not looking to create a nest but had already made one underneath the dining-room table.

He said I was very lucky as wasps will always find a way in and out of their nest and will chew through floorboards if that's what it takes. It was just as well my attempts to stop the wasps were so feeble otherwise the wasps would have eaten their way into the house to escape or, worse than that, any one of us could have ended up falling through the rotten floorboards into a flurry of buzzing and stinging.

GEORGE'S MUM IS A BIT OVER PROTECTIVE...

'I Want to Break Free'

It doesn't matter what you try to do to contain children, there comes a time when they will break free. The only choice you have is whether to let them grow into their freedom or fight their way out (in which case you'd better buy the boxing gloves now).

Letting children go doesn't happen overnight. You don't wake up one morning to discover their beds are empty and they've vanished into thin air leaving nothing behind but Blu-Tack on the walls where the posters of pop stars once were. Breaking free of your apron strings is a process which begins when children are tiny. From the moment they can crawl away from you they start to learn about independence and it's your job to teach them the right way to use it. The easiest way for you to let a child go is for you to prepare him for the future.

Top Tip: Children leaving home are a fact of life so aim to help them make it a smooth transition.

The better prepared he is, the happier you'll be about the prospect. Try and remember:

- Children need to learn to make their own decisions rather than always having to rely on someone else to make their choices for them. When they are still quite young it's a good idea to encourage them to make choices under your guidance. Doing this helps children to develop confidence and self-esteem. However well educated a child may be, if he can't interact with people confidently because he doesn't have the necessary social skills, he will find the adult world a much harder place.
- It is important to teach your child how to make informed rather than biased judgments. Help him to think through issues for himself rather than plumping for whatever appeals to him the most. Once your son or daughter is old enough to speak for themselves try not to answer for them – even if you don't agree with the views they express.

- Learn to guide gently without putting children down. Never tell them they're stupid or worthless. Everything you do should be geared towards them building up a positive self-image.
- Help your child to work out their own values system. You can't insist on the way your offspring think or behave but you can influence them for good. Recognise that as children grow up they may change their likes/dislikes and views, so don't go telling all their friends that their favourite food is Marmite soldiers when they're thirteen and prefer burgers and chips!
- Aim to show your child that the right decision in any situation is not always the easiest. The path of least resistance is not always the best. Life is hard and not always fair, and you do your child no favours if you bring them up to believe otherwise.

 Top Tip: Don't worry too much about your child making mistakes – there are times when he will have to get it wrong in order to learn.

To Boldly Go

This last point was brought home quite forcefully to our daughter Amy when she went on a French exchange with the school. The carrot on the end of the stick of this exchange was a trip to Euro Disney on the last day, so Amy, much to her siblings' envy, signed up. We let her go on the trip although we

153

had reservations. The trip wasn't quite what Amy had hoped for. Although she really enjoyed the days out with her school friends, she found living with a foreign family quite tough and was extremely homesick. Two days before the return journey she had already packed her bags – I can't imagine what Monsieur and Madame thought! Amy learnt a lot through her experience, however – far more than if we had insisted she didn't go on the trip because she might not have liked it. She learnt how to cope in a situation she was not happy with and she learnt what it means to be independent. When she arrived home, she was a tired and sorry sight. Although I suspect she wouldn't have gone had she known what it was really going to be like, Amy grew up a little bit more because of it. Her values have certainly changed – no longer is a trip to Euro Disney the 'be all and end all': she would have gladly forfeited that particular excursion in favour of the next bus home.

As is so often the case, the eldest or only child is the pathfinder, the pioneer, or the guinea pig, depending on your view. Both of you have to work a way through the maze that lies ahead. By the time another child has come along, mums are invariably more relaxed and have a better idea about what they are doing, even if they're still puzzled by much of their offspring's behaviour. When you've already loosened the apron strings for one child, subsequent children often find there's a little more slack in the rope.

Jelly Moulds

A key way to give your child self-confidence is to trust him. The more trust you put in your child, the more he will believe in himself and his ability. In the same way that you give your son or daughter the opportunity to make choices you should give them the opportunity to earn your trust. It's a sad truth that no matter what they do, some parents never trust their children. Trust means allowing your child to act freely within prescribed boundaries. For example, when teenagers start going out on their own, give them a set time to be back. This is not just so you know they're safe but also so they can prove to you they can handle your trust responsibly. Don't announce to their friends that there are certain things you would never let your son or daughter do. Give children the benefit of the doubt unless you have good reason to disbelieve them.

 Top Tip: *A good way to build up a child's self-confidence is by trusting him.*

Telling your child you trust them is empty unless you take action and show them you do. Start by trusting them with small things. One mum refused to let her teenage daughter wear make-up because she thought she'd paint her face with all sorts of strange colours. The daughter, on the other hand, didn't want any more than some mascara and lip gloss and had no intention of covering her face with make-up. All she wanted was to be allowed the same privileges as her friends. In effect, the mum was saying 'I don't trust you'. Be careful you don't assume that your son or daughter will do what you would do in the same situation!

It's important not to try and force your child into a mould based around your needs and expectations. While children need boundaries around them they also need room to grow – sometimes in a different direction to the way you would like! To put it in agricultural terms, if your child wants to be a lettuce, don't stick him in a vase and pretend he's a carnation – you won't be convinced and he won't be happy! Children are not there to achieve all the things that you couldn't. They are not simply extensions of their mum or dad – they're individuals in their own right. Don't insist they have violin lessons because you didn't get the chance to learn. You will regret it in more ways than one if they don't have the inclination and you have to listen to unenthusiastic renditions of 'Twinkle Twinkle Little Star' at school concerts. Neither should you sign them up for football coaching because you were a star player in your youth and still have the trophies to prove it.

It's important to encourage children as they struggle to find their way in life. Hanging onto them is another burden they can do without. As a mum, your Mission Impossible, 'should you choose to accept it', is to be a guiding hand, not one that hauls them back. Children are all different and will need slightly different guidance, but whatever their character, the target is to enable every child to be a mature independent adult.

Three of our children have sensible ideas of what they want to do when they are older. The careers they're aiming for are pretty much in line with their characters, but the youngest has gone off at a complete tangent. He has two aims in life. One is to be an ice-cream man. This is a very important job when you're six years old and you live with a mother who resorts to turning up the radio and singing very loudly whenever the Greensleeves jingle of the ice-cream van approaches. The other ambition is to have a verruca like his brother and sisters (this was inspired after we went through a difficult period of feet problems).

 Top Tip: *Aim to encourage children to grow in the way that suits their character – not yours.*

Inch Worm

Mums hold their children tightly because they are precious. One of the times this was drummed home forcefully was when Joseph was three years old. He was suffering from tonsillitis and I took him to the doctor for some antibiotics. When we got home Joseph was content to lie quietly on the settee. Mike was not yet home from work and I was in another room with a friend who had popped in. Suddenly Amy and Eleanor came rushing into the room in a terrible panic saying that something was wrong with Joseph. I ran into the lounge to discover him in a strangely contorted position and shaking. Unbeknown to me he was having a convulsion.

We rang for an ambulance and somehow I had the presence of mind to remove his outer clothes and start cooling him. The ambulance seemed to take an eternity and all I could do was keep sponging him down and pray that he would be all right. Eventually we arrived at the hospital and, after a nightmare of an evening, he was finally admitted to the children's ward. I spent the night sitting on the edge of his bed, trying to keep him cool and all the while watching for any flicker which might mean another fit. He recovered quickly but it took me much longer. Even now, several years on, I still feel the urge to panic at the slightest sign of Joseph's temperature rising. In fact, I feel the urge to panic if anyone I know looks a bit hot.

Giving children their independence little by little can be hard. Although you know when your child is ready to be a bit more responsible, when do you let your son or daughter walk home from school on their own? How late do you let them stay out? When do you give them the keys to your car? If ever? Find out what freedom other children the same age have been given, then trust your judgment. There are no universal answers, but a good dose of common sense helps. You *will* know.

Most of the decisions mums make to encourage their children to become a bit more independent are riddled with that monster 'Worry'. When Katie was in her last year at primary school she had the opportunity to take her Cycling Proficiency Test. Katie was not the most confident of riders and somehow her mum, Debbie, had to get the bike to school every day for a week. The bike wouldn't fit in the car and so the only solution was for Katie to ride it, very carefully along side streets, to school. Debbie couldn't bear the prospect of her daughter wobbling along without supervision so she decided to drive along slowly, just behind, and keep an eye on her. Quite what good she thought this would do she had no idea, but it made her feel better. Debbie had the trauma of watching Katie wobble all the way to school for a whole week. Her cycling improved as the week went on, but not before she had lost a pedal and run over the examiner's toes. Somehow, by the end of the week, she had improved enough to pass the test, which to her mother's mind was a miracle!

Debbie's strange driving habits were repeated a few months later as the prospect of secondary school loomed ahead of her and her daughter. Katie had to get the bus to school, so before term began Debbie thought it would be a good idea for her to have a 'dummy' run. This meant getting a bus to school during the holidays. Katie, of course, had no trouble getting on the correct bus for what was a very simple journey: Debbie had more trouble as she drove after it down the hill, stopping a short distance away from every bus stop. An elderly gentleman spoke to Katie on the bus as he couldn't help but notice the blue car which was following with a strange woman inside. She seemed to be kerb crawling behind the bus, smiling and waving encouragingly for the best part of three miles. Needless to say, Katie got off at the correct stop, where her mum pulled up and took her back home.

Top Tip: *Try to prepare yourself well in advance for the day your child leaves home.*

Holding Back the Years

It's often harder for mums than dads to wave goodbye to a son or daughter as they leave to set up home on their own, or go off to college. Mums are usually the prime carers – the ones that children spend the most time with. As such they're much

more involved in the nitty gritty everyday workings of children's lives. The void which is left behind is not so easy to fill. But look on the bright side. Friends with children who have already flown the nest say it's wonderful to have some space and a house that stays tidy. Think how great it will be when you aren't forever chasing half the contents of your home as they migrate into your teenager's bedroom. And a house that isn't littered with size 8 smelly trainers is close to heaven. The peace and quiet of a house without young adults gives you the chance to play *your* choice of music without competition. Some mums whose children have left home tell me that once they've got used to a different life, they don't want the kids back! They want the space and the freedom to do all the things they've been putting off. I've been amazed to hear just how short that transition period can be – a few weeks rather than months.

There are ways you can prepare yourself, however, for the moment your son or daughter leaves home:

- Create a memory box. Although you won't have room in the house for all those spidery drawings which say 'Mum', save some to put away in a box. Maybe some baby clothes as well – the ones you especially liked and can't bear to throw away. Keep tickets from special days out, snippets of baby hair or the odd pressed flower with a record of who gave it to you and when. Put anything in the box which brings back treasured memories for you as your child grows up (my children wanted to put their milk teeth in the box, but I thought that a bit gruesome).

- If you're good with a needle, save some of your child's clothes and turn them into a patchwork quilt. Woolly jumpers don't work very well, but cotton dresses or shirts are ideal.

- Keep a written record of your son's or daughter's development. When they walked, talked, who their best friends were etc.

- Keep a record of the weird and wonderful things your child says and does. It's incredible how you forget so much – all the funny words and phrases children use. You think they'll be forever stapled in your mind, but unless you write them down, they work themselves free and slip away. Rifling through old diaries I found the word 'temtoot' which was Eleanor's word for elephant. Had I not written it down, I may well have forgotten.

- Take the time now to name and date photos. Even if you only scribble where and when on the back it'll save you

161

scratching your head some time in the future when you're trying to work out the picture's significance.

- Keep a journal of how you're feeling. You needn't write/draw something every day, just when you feel like it. Neither does it have to be a work of literary genius. It's a reminder to you of your life with children.

When I'm Sixty-Four

We all know stories of children who never leave home and devote their lives to their parents only to be left isolated and alone in middle age when their parents die. And while devotion and loyalty is to be commended in any child, no son or daughter should take up the entire burden of their parents' life for them.

Katherine grew up in a home where she was over-protected. Her mother loved her dearly and in her efforts to demonstrate this to her daughter she became quite possessive. When Katherine had children of her own she was quite determined not to be an over-protective mother to her children. She knew exactly what the signs and symptoms were and set out early on to encourage her children to stand on their own two feet. One day when her son Adam was about seven he told his mum that he loved her and was going to live at home for ever and ever. Katherine responded to this by telling her son that one day, when he was a lot older, he might want to move away from home and that he didn't have to stay with her for ever. She went on to explain that he might not even want to stay in the same town, or the same part of the country, and getting more and more carried away, she told him that he might not even want to stay in the same country – he might find he wanted to live somewhere like . . . Australia. With this Adam burst into tears and sobbed, 'But I don't want to live in Australia!' So build in independence but try not to over-compensate!

Mums have the ability to go to one extreme or another. Not only are there those who can't bear to let their children go, who hang on to them tight, but there are those who tell their children that once they get to sixteen or eighteen they've got to leave home and make their own way in the world. Most of us would agree that the best idea is not to boot them out but encourage them to be independent enough to fly the nest when they're ready. Birds are a good analogy. Parent birds don't stuff little gaping beaks full of food until they're fed up and hoist the chicks over the edge with a sharp peck. Instead they keep going until the chicks are ready to fledge.

 Top Tip: *Aim to strike a happy balance between being over-protective and so laid back that you fall off the caring scale!*

When it comes to letting children go, try to work on the basis that you won't be losing your children for good, but you'll be part of a growing, maturing relationship. Hopefully you'll become less of an authority figure and more of a friend. Seeing your son or daughter successfully carving their own individual way through life should be enough to convince you that you didn't do too badly after all and that they survived in spite of your mistakes! And there is always the prospect of future grandchildren to console those who can't bear the thought of not having small children swinging on their ears all the time.

Our youngest son Joseph takes an alternative approach to the prospect of leaving home. He recently suggested to me that when he's older he should continue to live in the house while Mum and Dad move out. Where to? Anywhere, he said. A rest home for dazed and confused parents perhaps? Or maybe he'll just put us in a field and leave us quietly to reflect on what we could have done better.

Further Information

Organisations

Parentalk
PO Box 23142
London SE1 0ZT

Tel: 0700 2000 500
Fax: 020 7450 9060
e-mail: pa.rentalk@virgin.net

Provides a range of resources and services designed to inspire parents to enjoy parenthood.

Care for the Family
Garth House, Leon Avenue
Cardiff CF4 7RG

Tel: 01222 811733
Fax: 01222 814089
e-mail: care.for.the.family@dial.
pipex.com
Web site: www.care-for-the-family.
org.uk

Providing support for families through seminars, resources and special projects.

Gingerbread
16–17 Clerkenwell Close
London EC1R 0AA

Tel: 020 7336 8183
Fax: 020 7336 8185
e-mail: office@gingerbread.org.uk
Web site: www.gingerbread.org.uk

Provides day-to-day support and practical help for lone parents.

Home-Start UK
2 Salisbury Road
Leicester LE1 7QR

Tel: 0116 2339 955
Fax: 0116 2330 232
e-mail: Enquiries@Homestarthq.
freeserve.co.uk

Committed to promoting the welfare of families with at least one child under five.

Kidscape
2 Grosvenor Gardens
London SW1W 0DH

Tel: 020 7730 3300
Fax: 020 7730 7081
e-mail: @kidscape.org.uk
Web site: www.kidscape.org.uk

Works to prevent the abuse of children through education programmes involving parents and teachers, providing a range of resources. Also runs a bullying helpline.

Maternity Alliance
45 Beech Street
London EC2P 2LX

Tel: 020 7588 8583
Fax: 020 7588 8584
e-mail: info@maternityalliance.org.uk

An independent national charity, working to improve rights and services for all pregnant women, new parents and their babies.

Meet-A-Mum Association (MAMA)
26 Avenue Road
London SE25 4DX

Tel: 020 8771 5595
Fax: 020 8239 1152
e-mail: meet-a-mum.assoc@cableinet.co.uk
Website: www.mama.org.uk

Helps mums who are feeling lonely, isolated or depressed by putting them in touch with other mums living nearby for friendship and support.

National Association for Maternal and Child Welfare
40–42 Osnaburgh Street
London NW1 3ND

Tel: 020 7383 4117/4541
Fax: 020 7383 4115
e-mail: valerie.sarebrothernamcw @btinternet.com
Website: www.charitynet.org-namcw

Telephone advice on childcare and family life.

National Council for One Parent Families
255 Kentish Town Road
London NW5 2LX

Lone Parent Line: 0800 018 5026
Maintenance & Money Line: 020 7428 5424
(Mon & Fri 10.30 a.m.–1.30 p.m; Wed 3–6 p.m.)

Information service for lone parents.

National Childbirth Trust (NCT)
Alexandra House
Oldham Terrace
London W3 6NH

Tel: 020 8992 8637
Fax: 020 8992 5929
Web site: www.nct-online.org

Information and support for expectant and pre-school parents.

National Drugs Helpline
0800 77 66 00
c/o Health Education Authority
Trevelyan House
30 Great Peter Street
London SW1P 2HW

Free helpline offering confidential advice. Can also send out free leaflets and answer any queries callers might have.

Positive Parenting Publications
1st Floor, 2A South Street
Gosport PO12 1ES

Tel: 01705 528787
Fax: 01705 501111
e-mail: info@parenting.org.uk
Web site: www.parenting.org.uk

Aims to prepare people for the role of parenting by helping parents, those about to become parents and also those who lead parenting groups.

Parent Network
Room 2, Winchester House
Kennington Park
11 Cranmer Road
London SW9 6EJ

Tel: 020 7735 1214
Fax: 020 7735 4692
e-mail: info@parentnetwork.
demon.co.uk

Provides support and education groups for parents in local communities.

Parentline
3rd Floor Chapel House
18 Hatton Place
London EC1N 8RU

Helpline: 0808 800 2222
Tel: 020 7209 2460
Fax: 020 7209 2461
e-mail: headoffice@parentlineplus.
org.uk
Web site: www.parentlineplus.org.uk

Provides a confidential telephone helpline for anyone in a parenting role including step-parents and those undergoing family change. Parentline is a Freephone service run by Parentline Plus.

Relate: National Marriage Guidance
National Headquarters
Herbert Gray College
Little Church Street
Rugby, Warwickshire CV21 3AP

Tel: 01788 573241
Fax: 01788 535007
e-mail: enquiries@national.relate.
org.uk
Web site: www.relate.org.uk

YouthNet UK
e-mail: youthnet@thesite.org.uk
Web site: www.thesite.org.uk

Aims to give young people access via the Internet to the most comprehensive information available.

Publications

The Sixty Minute Mother, Rob Parsons, Hodder & Stoughton
The Parentalk Guide to the Toddler Years, Steve Chalke, Hodder & Stoughton
The Parentalk Guide to the Childhood Years, Steve Chalke, Hodder & Stoughton
The Parentalk Guide to the Teenage Years, Steve Chalke, Hodder & Stoughton
How to Succeed as a Parent, Steve Chalke, Hodder & Stoughton
Sex Matters, Steve Chalke and Nick Page, Hodder & Stoughton
Positive Parenting: Raising Children with Self-Esteem, E. Hartley-Brewer, Mandarin Paperback
Raising Boys, Steve Biddulph, Thorsons
The Secret of Happy Children, Steve Biddulph, Thorsons
Families and How to Survive Them, Skinner and Cleese, Vermilion
Stress Free Parenting, Dr David Haslam, Vermilion
How Not to be a Perfect Mother, Libby Purves, HarperCollins

Parenting Courses

- **Parentalk Parenting Course** A new parenting course designed to give parents the opportunity to share their experiences, learn from each other and discover some principles of parenting.

  Parentalk
  PO Box 23142
  London SE1 0ZT
  For more information phone 0700 2000 500

- **Parent Network** Operates through self-help groups run by parents for parents known as Parent-Link. The groups are mostly run for 2 or more hours, over 13 weekly sessions. For more information phone 020 7735 1214.

- **Positive Parenting Publications** Publish a range of low cost, easy to read, common sense resource materials which provide help, information and advice. Responsible for running a range of parenting courses across the UK. For more information phone 01705 528787.